THE
UNHEEDED
CHRIST

With our love
& With every good wish
for 2009 + beyond.

William + Carine

DAVID COOK

THE
UNHEEDED
CHRIST

DAVID COOK

ISBN 978-1-84550-369-7

Copyright © David Cook 2008

10 9 8 7 6 5 4 3 2 1

Published in 2008
by
Christian Focus Publications, Ltd.,
Geanies House, Fearn, Ross-shire,
IV20 1TW, Great Britain.

www.christianfocus.com

Cover design by Moose77.com

Printed and bound in Denmark by Norhaven

CONTENTS

For Maxine

'Her children arise and call her blessed;
her husband also...'

INTRODUCTION

The talks in this book have been transcribed and edited from David Cook's sermons given at 'Principal's Hour', Sydney Missionary and Bible College.

David shares freely about his day-to-day and personal family life. His speech is conversational and often passionate – which at times can be difficult to adequately replicate in the written format. It is important to note that not captured in this book were his prayers before and following each sermon.

Jesus Christ is a provocative, uncompromising teacher. Yet it's easy to become so accustomed to Jesus' words that they become old friends – comfortable and familiar and unchallenging. We can get so used to Him that we forget to take notice and heed His commands. When we read the Gospels as twenty-first-century citizens of God's kingdom, are we also living out His words in radical Christian discipleship?

In a series of thirteen talks, David Cook takes us through a selection of Jesus' teaching from the Gospel of Matthew. Jesus demands serious obedience from His people in all areas of life, and challenges us about crucial issues such as:

- loving enemies
- forgiveness
- sex
- ambition
- adultery
- wealth accumulation
- revenge
- the reality of judgment
- resolving tension between Christians
- self-delusion

This book will challenge you, as you hear freshly the words of Christ. Jesus is the Lord: listen to Him again, and don't let Him go unheeded.

CHAPTER ONE

LOVE YOUR ENEMIES

MATTHEW 5:43-48

In Matthew's Gospel, chapter 5, verses 43-48, our Lord Jesus continues what is known as the *Sermon on the Mount*.

> [43]You have heard that it was said, 'Love your neighbour and hate your enemy.' [44]But I tell you: Love your enemies and pray for those who persecute you, [45]that you may be sons of your Father in heaven. He causes his sun to rise on the evil and the good, and sends rain on the righteous and the unrighteous. [46]If you love those who love you, what reward will you get? Are not even the tax collectors doing that? [47]And if you greet only your brothers, what are you doing more than others? Do not even pagans do that? [48]Be perfect, therefore, as your heavenly Father is perfect.

In his book, *The 100: A Ranking of the Most Influential Persons in History,*[1] Michael Hart is careful to explain that this is not a ranking of those he considers to be the best people in history, or the greatest people in history. Rather, he provides a ranking of the

---

[1] Michael H Hart, *The 100: A Ranking of the Most Influential Persons in History*, London: Simon & Schuster, 1993.

most influential people in history. Number 1, *the* most influential person in history, is not Jesus. The second most influential person is not Jesus. The third most influential person in history, according to Michael Hart, is Jesus Christ. Why has Jesus been supplanted from the first position, the most influential position that we probably think He should have? To whom has Hart given the number-one position? Hart, who claims to be neither a Muslim nor a Christian, has put Mohammed first because in his observation of Muslims and Christians, Mohammed has far more influence over the lives of Muslims than Jesus Christ does over the lives of Christians.

This is a challenging point for us, because Hart is talking about Jesus Christ's lack of influence on *Christians*. He is not talking about Jesus Christ's lack of influence on unbelievers. What he is saying is that Christians, from his observation, do not widely follow, believe or take heed of their Lord and Master, Jesus Christ.

I have thought about this and have battled with an adjective for this series of meditations. I've been looking for the opposite of 'influential'. 'The Uninfluential Christ'? 'The Disregarded Christ'? But I finally settled for the title, 'The Unheeded Christ'.

Starting with the illustration that Michael Hart gives, the prime example of the Christian's failure to be influenced by the teaching of Jesus Christ is in Matthew, chapter 5, verses 43-48. Verse 48 is a summary of the *Sermon on the Mount* to this point. The Lord Jesus says, 'Be perfect, therefore, as your heavenly Father is perfect.' We are to be perfect, or mature, like God our Heavenly Father is perfect or mature.

What is the way of maturity? How does a boy become a man? What is Hollywood's answer to this question? A film I saw many years ago is typical of Hollywood's response. You take the young man and stand him before a building. You say, 'If he goes in there and experiences everything that building has to offer, he'll come out a man.' And indeed, the young man, who is 16 years of age, is taken to the owner of the building. The request is: 'I give you the boy, you give me the man.' What is this building? It's a saloon, and in the saloon there is a brothel. What turns the boy into a man according to Hollywood? Whisky, cigars and illicit sexual activity. That's the way of maturity according to Hollywood.

What is the way a boy becomes a man and a girl becomes a woman? What's the way of completion, what's the way of maturity, according to our Lord Jesus? Earlier in Matthew, chapter 5, verse 21, Jesus says, 'Do not murder. But understand also that a form of murdering is anger and slander.' The world says it is all right to hate a little bit, and a word here or there never hurt anyone. But the Lord Jesus says that reconciliation and communication must be kept open. Consider chapter 5, verses 27 and 28.

> [27]You have heard that it was said, 'Do not commit adultery.'
> [28]But I tell you that anyone who looks at a woman lustfully has already committed adultery with her in his heart.

Jesus says that adultery both in practice and *in the mind* is to be avoided. But we can't escape it. If you go to the movies, see a DVD or surf the net, you are always going to see something that encourages desirous, lustful thoughts. Jesus says we must resist lust like death itself. Verses 31 and 32 read as follows:

> [31]It has been said, 'Anyone who divorces his wife must give her a certificate of divorce.' [32]But I tell you that anyone who divorces his wife, except for marital unfaithfulness, causes her to become an adulteress, and anyone who marries the divorced woman commits adultery.

Jesus says that there is no right to divorce. There are very limited grounds for divorce allowed here, and even then it's not a right. Yet divorce is so common in our society where marriage is put at the mercy of feelings of love. Jesus says, resist unfaithfulness. Look at chapter 5, verses 33-37.

[33]Again, you have heard that it was said to the people long ago, 'Do not break your oath, but keep the oaths you have made to the Lord.' [34]But I tell you, Do not swear at all: either by heaven, for it is God's throne; [35]or by the earth, for it is his footstool; or by Jerusalem, for it is the city of the Great King. [36]And do not swear by your head, for you cannot make even one hair white or black. [37]Simply let your 'Yes' be 'Yes,' and your 'No,' 'No'; anything beyond this comes from the evil one.

As to oaths, let your 'Yes' be 'Yes' and your 'No' be 'No'. Don't break your word. In our society, words mean nothing until there is a signed legal agreement in triplicate. Jesus says, 'No'. Who is the man whom God admires? It is the one 'who swears to his own hurt but abides by his promise'.[2] In chapter 5, verses 38 and 39, Jesus says,

[38]You have heard that it was said, 'Eye for eye, and tooth for tooth.' [39]But I tell you, Do not resist an evil person. If someone strikes you on the right cheek, turn to him the other also.

There is to be no revenge or defensiveness. In contemporary society, legal rights are a way of life. Litigation is a normal way even for some Christians. Jesus says no, that is not the way of maturity. And all of this teaching culminates in verses 43-45, in which He tells us that we are to love our enemies and pray for our persecutors. Martyn Lloyd-Jones describes this as the most unique Christian commandment.

[43]You have heard that it was said, 'Love your neighbour and hate your enemy.' [44]But I tell you: Love your enemies and pray for those who persecute you, [45]that you may be sons of your Father in heaven. He causes the sun to rise on the evil and the good, and sends rain on the righteous and the unrighteous.

---

[2] Psalm 15:4b.

All of these are descriptions of the way of maturity for the citizen of God's kingdom.

In this last section of the passage Jesus starts with a contrast in verse 43. 'You have heard that it was said, "Love your neighbour and hate your enemy"'. We know that the scribes, the Jewish leaders, said that. If you are coming along the road and you see a neighbour's ox bogged in the mud, you get that ox out of the mud, provided it is your neighbour's ox and provided, of course, that it belongs to a fellow Jew. If it belongs to a Gentile, you disregard the ox altogether. In other words, the scribes said, 'Love your neighbour (that is, your fellow Jew), but you can disregard the needs of Gentiles and hate the Gentiles, who are your enemies.' Jesus says, 'But I tell you, no!' This is a truly distinctive teaching.

Notice, first, the command and the reason Jesus gives for it. The command comes in verse 44. 'Love your enemies and pray for those who persecute you.' Who then are our enemies? They could be national or political enemies. They could be those who persecute us because of our faith. They could be those with whom we have difficult relationships. What is to be our attitude to them? Look at verse 39. First of all, it is to be passive; that is, we are not to retaliate or try to get back at them. But Jesus goes further. He says our attitude is also to be active, verse 43: You are to do good to your enemies. You are to love them. And you are to pray for your enemies. Why should we act in such a surprising way? Verse 45 tells us: So that the fact you are God's child will be obvious, because God likewise is generous and kind without distinction.

In Wee Waa, our first country parish in New South Wales,[3] there were Christian farmers and there were non-Christian farmers. When it rained and when the sun shone, it rained and shone on the Christian farms and the non-Christian farms! What a chaotic thing it would be if the rain only fell and the sun only shone on the Christian farms. There would be chaos

---

[3] Australia's most populous state.

in the created order. There would also be chaos in the world of relationships if we Christians only loved our friends, if we only returned love for love, if we only prayed for those who were our friends and ignored our enemies. How does God love? He loves because He *is* love. He doesn't love because we are lovable. This is not a deserved love, it is a gracious love. God is generous to all. When you love your enemy, you are showing that it is 'like Father, like child'. You are acting in a godly way, in a God-like way; you are giving love without discrimination.

Now why is this generally not practised? I think we would all say it is because it is an ideal. Because it is so contrary to our nature, we find it very hard to do.

There are three things I find helpful in the battle to love my enemies.

The *first* is to shed self-protection; to shed self-defensiveness. The way I respond to you should not be conditioned by your acceptance of me. As a Christian, I will not allow another person who is unpleasant to me to compromise my Christian walk by causing me to react to them in the same way that they have treated me. I must detach myself from self-justifying, self-protecting ways. The Lord Jesus says that I am to be generous, gracious, and unconditional: to love, no matter what is coming my way.

The *second* thing that is helpful is to remember the words of the apostle Paul, that our battle is not against flesh and blood.[4] Our enemies are not simply those we see. We know that behind our enemies stands the devil himself. That is the level of our battle: It is at a spiritual level. It is against the devil, not against people.

And *thirdly*, it is important that we give thanks to almighty God, both for the friends he has given us and for the enemies he has given us. Our enemies are giving us opportunities to show our heavenly rebirth.

---

[4] Ephesians 6:12

Consider again what Jesus says in verse 44:

> But I tell you: Love your enemies and pray for those who
> persecute you ...

He says we are to 'love' and 'pray'. But sometimes we feel we
can only pray. Jesus prayed, 'Father, forgive them' as they were
putting Him to death.[5] Stephen said, 'Don't hold this sin against
them.'[6] Notice again what Jesus says. Look at verse 44. 'Love your
enemies' – we love our friends – 'and pray for your persecutors'.
We pray for the persecut*ed*. But do we pray for the persecut*or*?
Now, you may say, 'It's far too hard to love my enemies when I
don't even like them!' But it really depends on what the Lord
Jesus means here by 'love' and what we understand 'love' to be.

I read a case study involving an interaction between a pastor
and a married couple. The couple had come to the pastor to tell
him they were getting a divorce because they no longer loved
one another. What they *really* came for, however, was his seal of
approval on their divorce.

'We've come to tell you we are getting a divorce.'

'Why are you getting a divorce?'

'Because we no longer love one another.'

'Well then, you should repent and learn to love one another
again.'

Their response? 'But we just don't feel any love for one
another and we are not going to be hypocrites and live together
under these conditions.'

The pastor then turned his attention to the husband and said,
'You are a professing Christian. The Bible tells you that you are to
love your wife, that you are to love your neighbour, and that you
are to love your enemies. However you categorise this woman,
you are to love her!'

---

[5] Luke 23:34
[6] Acts 7:60

In other words, love is not feelings first. Love is action. Jesus is not saying, 'Feel nice things about your enemies.' He is saying, 'Move towards them in ways that are good.' Isn't that consistent with what Jesus said to the Ephesian church in Revelation 2? 'You've lost your first love.' Therefore, He says, 'Repent and **do** the things you did at first!'[7] He doesn't tell them to change their feelings. He says, in effect, 'Don't repent and *feel* for me in the same way as you did before, but repent and **do** the things which you did at first.' Feelings inevitably follow actions.

Love, therefore, is not primarily emotion. According to these verses it is praying and acting for the good of the other. At that point, our enemies provide great opportunities to show forth that we have a heavenly birth.[8]

In Romans chapter 12, verses 14 and 15, we see how the apostle Paul brings out this same teaching in the letter to the Roman congregation.

> Bless those who persecute you; bless and do not curse. Rejoice with those who rejoice; mourn with those who mourn.

Now the very opposite is often true, isn't it? When my enemy is rejoicing, I am mourning. When my enemy is mourning, I am happy. But these verses turn that way of thinking upside down. The apostle Paul says, 'When they rejoice, you rejoice with them. When they're weeping, you weep with them. Bless, don't curse.'[9] We need to find creative ways of being loving to our enemies.

The lecture building on our campus was completed in 1998. During the years leading up to its completion, there was a great deal of opposition to it from some in the local neighbourhood. At that time we happened to have passionfruit vines growing over our back fence. The passionfruit would ripen in December and January, usually when I was away at Katoomba for Christian

---

[7] Revelation 2:4-5
[8] Matthew 5:45
[9] Romans 12:14-15

youth conventions. My wife Maxine would pick the passionfruit and put them in the freezer. On a hot day you could take the frozen passionfruit and eat it. It was terrific. One particular year, I came home from January convention, and when I noticed there were no passionfruit on the vine, I thought, 'Oh, they are in the freezer. Terrific!' I went to the freezer but they weren't there either.

'Where are the passionfruit?'

Maxine said, 'I packed them into plastic bags and took them to our neighbours.'

I said, 'To *all* of our neighbours?'

'Yes, and I also invited them to our church mission.'

Now that's surprising, isn't it? Unexpected generosity shown in response to opposition. Remarkably, through various events in the last few years, God has enabled that local community relationship to be extended. But there needed to be that first step of responding with the surprising demonstration of creative love in the face of difficult relationships.

Some people regard leaders within their own denominations as spiritual enemies. This has happened in my own denomination. I need to remember to pray for my spiritual opponents: to ask God to give me opportunities to do good to them. I always need to pray, when I am fighting any battle for the truth, that God will deliver me from underhanded, personal, vindictive ways; because the struggle is in the name of the Saviour who says, in Matthew, chapter 5, verse 44, '... But I tell you ...' Very often when we are fighting for the truth, we can get quite antagonistic and forget these words of Jesus, '... But I tell you, love your enemies and pray for those who persecute you ...'.

Now, let's consider verses 46 and 47. I want to discuss true subversion, true revolution. There is an old saying, 'If you're not a socialist by twenty, you've got no heart. If you're not a capitalist by thirty, you've got no brain.' I'm sure many people during university days are quite left-wing. Then by the time they've got a mortgage, in their thirties, they've become right-wing! They soon lose their old ideals. It is interesting even now to listen to the old left-wingers in our society – people like Gough Whitlam[10] and Tom Uren[11]. (Gough Whitlam still calls his fellow Labor Party people 'comrades'. It's a lovely way of talking.) But what's interesting about the Marxist revolutionaries (I'm not implying Gough Whitlam is a Marxist revolutionary!) is that Marx taught his fellow revolutionaries to love the comrades, but to hate the class enemy. That is the way of revolution. You love the 'in' group, but you hate the 'outside' group. It is all so typical of the world.

Reflect again on verses 46 and 47.

> [46]If you love those who love you, what reward will you get? Are not even the tax collectors doing that? [47]And if you greet only your brothers, what are you doing more than others? Do not even pagans do that?

It is so typical of the tax collectors and pagans that they love in a limited way. They love only their friends. But Jesus is saying, 'If you want to be a true revolutionary, go against the flow. Be involved in truly subversive activity; be truly mature, don't just love each other, but love your enemies as well. Don't just greet those who greet you, but greet those who ignore you and show their contempt for you.'

I have been reading of churches in the United States which, in the past, have been heavily involved in the politics of the Moral Majority movement. One pastor said, 'We now realise that the nature of politics is that it divides communities. We've turned our backs on all forms of politics. We don't even go marching for Jesus. Instead we have given ourselves to speaking the truth accompanied by radical acts of love and compassion to all people, no matter what their attitude is to us.' Now, friends, that is what authentic discipleship is. It is *seen*. The highest test

---

[10] Former Prime Minister of Australia.
[11] Former Politician and Minister of Australian Labor Party with Whitlam.

of our integrity, of our faith and our maturity, is how we treat those who dislike us.

To return evil for evil is so normal, so human. And to return good for good, is normal; it is human. To return evil for good is devilish. But to return good in the face of evil – this is the way of godliness. Dietrich Bonhoeffer, a theologian, who was put to death in Nazi Germany under Hitler, said that the cross is the great differential of our faith. The cross drives the Christian faith. What you see at the cross is that the Son of God gives His life. He gives His life for sinners. He gives His life for those who are powerless. He gives His life for the ungodly. He gives His life for His enemies. That is the differential which drives us: love for the unlovable, love for the unloving.

Contemplate what Hart says at the end of his opening chapter. He refers to Jesus' injunction to love our enemies.

These are surely among the most remarkable and original ethical ideas ever presented. If they were widely followed I would have no hesitation in placing Jesus first in this book. But the truth is that they are not widely followed. Indeed, they are not even actually generally accepted. Most Christians consider the injunction to love your enemy as at most an ideal which might be realised in some perfect world, but one which is not a reasonable guide to conduct in the actual world we live in. We do not normally practise love for our enemies, we do not expect others to practise it, we do not teach our children to practise it. Jesus' most distinctive teaching therefore remains an intriguing but basically untried suggestion.[12]

Love your enemies.

I would have liked Michael Hart to meet Betsy Ten Boom as she was dying in a Nazi concentration camp. Her testimony revealed that no matter how deep the pit of hatred and anger is, God's love is deeper. I would like him to interview Gladys

---

[12]Michael Hart, *The 100*, p.20-21.

Staines, whose husband, Graham, and two young sons, Phillip and Timothy, were torched to death in 1999 in Orissa State in India. She went back with her sole surviving daughter to the leprosy mission to heal, and to minister to, some of the very people who were responsible for the hatred that led to the torching of her two sons and her husband. That is surprising; that is impressive. That is the way of maturity, perfection and completion, according to the Lord Jesus. I would like Michael Hart to meet Gladys Staines.

Who are your enemies? Who are the people who consider you as an ememy? Who are the people who show contempt for you? Who are the people you find hard to love? Spend some time now in silence to pray for just one of them. As you pray, ask God to give you opportunities to move towards that person to do good, that God will strengthen you so that you will not allow yourself to be compromised by their antagonistic attitude to you. Pray also that you will be unfailingly kind and generous to them, as your heavenly Father is kind and generous to you.

CHAPTER TWO

DO NOT RESIST

MATTHEW 5:38-42

[38]You have heard that it was said, 'Eye for eye, and tooth for tooth.' [39]But I tell you, Do not resist an evil person. If someone strikes you on the right cheek, turn to him the other also. [40]And if someone wants to sue you and take your tunic, let him have your cloak as well. [41]If someone forces you to go one mile, go with him two miles. [42]Give to the one who asks you, and do not turn away from the one who wants to borrow from you (Matt. 5:38-42)

I was raised in Sydney, in the 1950s and 1960s. My parents bought our first television, which was a 17-inch Stromberg Carlson, in 1959. It gave me *Disneyland*, *Hopalong Cassidy*, *Bonanza*, the *Mickey Mouse Club*, and *Gunsmoke* – a staple daily diet of good old American culture. Today, of course, television is far more sophisticated but it is no less American. *Law and Order*, *LA Law* and *The Practice* are among my favourite TV shows. It was once said that Australia was some 10 years behind the United States, so whatever is happening in the United States today, will, in 10 years' time, happen in Australia. Nowadays, I think, this time lag is much shorter. Australian culture today is more and more reflecting American culture – a society in which we are increasingly litigious, and aware of our legal rights.

At the gym recently, I met a teacher in his early sixties. He was telling me that all his teaching life he had been engaged in the private tutoring of boys. But this year, for the first time, he was no longer taking this role.

'Why not?' I asked, knowing him to be a very good teacher.

He replied, 'Because now I know that if a boy I tutor makes an allegation against me, I'm guilty until proven innocent, and it would be almost impossible to prove my innocence.'

I know of a missionary who is suing a missionary society. I also know of a denomination that is currently suing one of its clergy. It is not unusual, for Christians to be involved in litigation against their employers, against institutions, even against Christian institutions and against other Christians. Being in ministry requires us to be as shrewd as a serpent and as gentle as a dove.

This chapter was very difficult to prepare because I constantly found myself wanting to qualify the teaching of Jesus. I wanted to qualify what Jesus was saying to a point where His message lost its bite! Basically, I could have written it in a way that justified the idea that we don't have to pay any attention to it. No wonder F. F. Bruce, when he wrote about these particular teachings of Jesus, called his book *The Hard Sayings of Jesus*[1].

These teachings of Jesus are so counter to the trends in our society that we want to qualify them out of existence. That is, when I am wronged I want to hit back, to retaliate. When this happens, Jesus becomes the unheeded Christ. So what is the appropriate response when I am wronged? It is the response in verses 38-42. Notice the familiar pattern in the Sermon on the Mount. Verse 38: 'You have heard.' Verse 39: 'But I tell you.' And then in verses 40-42, Jesus gives two examples of the Christian response.

---

[1] F. F. Bruce, *The Hard Sayings of Jesus*, Hodder & Stoughton, 1998.

Notice how the pattern begins in verse 38: 'You have heard that it was said, "Eye for eye and tooth for tooth."'

That is a quotation from Exodus, Leviticus and Deuteronomy. It seems cruel, doesn't it? You gouge out my eye, then I can have your eye gouged out! But this law was designed to be restrictive, to prevent ongoing blood feuds. It was designed to limit the problem of payback. It is interesting to note, too, that these laws were given to the judges of Israel so that those in Israel's judicial system could establish justice in the land. And before long in Israel, money could be paid instead of an eye. So compensation replaced the whole idea of the literal retaliation of an eye for an eye and a tooth for a tooth. Yet this statement has been used to justify all sorts of malice and vengeance.

Bear in mind, however, what Jesus says in verse 39: 'But I tell you ...' In the kingdom of Jesus, do not resist evil. Do not set yourself against the evil person. If he strikes you on the right cheek, turn to him the left also. We are told elsewhere, in James 4:7, that we are not to resist God, but we are to resist the devil. The Lord Jesus tells us literally that we are not to resist evil; we are not to stand up against evil. (In the original Greek in Matthew, the verb is 'antitassomai', to range in battle against, resist.) Do not stand against the evil man. Jesus' followers are not to retaliate.

Martin Luther took this literally. When he found lice nibbling through his hair, he believed they were evil and that it was wrong for him to resist them. So he just let the lice stay and nibble through his hair. But when he married Catherine von Baurer, she wasn't prepared to put up with it! So Luther developed a much more down-to-earth and realistic approach to the issue.

What is Jesus saying in this passage? Is He saying there is to be no resistance to evil? That is, we should have no police? Is he saying that if you are a Christian, you should not be a policeman? That you cannot be a judge? A soldier? That you cannot be involved in prison work? No, Jesus cannot be encouraging evil or injustice. Then what is He saying here? Is He saying, 'Resist personal revenge'? John Stott says Jesus is not prohibiting justice, but he is prohibiting us taking the law into our own hands.[2]

In verses 40-42, there are four examples addressed to you – singular 'you', not a group. When confronted with evil, you must not retaliate. Rather, you must be detached and not allow your behaviour to be determined by the behaviour that is directed towards you. You cannot allow your response to be determined by the antagonism that comes to you. Jesus, of course, is the example of that. Peter says in 1 Peter 2:21, 'To this you were called, because Christ suffered for you, leaving you an example, that you should follow in his steps.' What an extraordinary example!

A songwriter said:

> On the cross he could have called ten thousand angels
> To destroy the world and set him free.
> He could have called ten thousand angels
> But he died alone for you and me.

And Peter says this is an example of non-retaliation for all Christ's people.

So there is a difference between how the judiciary is to act and how I am to react as a disciple of Jesus. Look at chapter 5, verse 48. 'Be perfect ... as your heavenly Father is perfect.' And chapter 5, verses 13 and 14: 'You are salt ... You are light.' The Lord Jesus knows that people will be evil, and there is a sense in which we need to leave revenge to almighty God. On a cosmic level, a universal level, God Himself will bring about eye for eye, and tooth for tooth.

How will justice come about? Paul takes up this teaching of Jesus in Romans. The apostle says in Romans 12:17-21:

> [17]Do not repay anyone evil for evil. Be careful to do what is right in the eyes of everybody. [18]If it is possible, as far as it

---

[2] John R. W. Stott, *Christian Counter-Culture: The Message of the Sermon on the Mount*, Inter Varsity Press, 1985.

depends on you, live at peace with everyone. [19]Do not take revenge, my friends, but leave room for God's wrath, for it is written: 'It is mine to avenge; I will repay,' says the Lord. [20]On the contrary:

'If your enemy is hungry, feed him;
    If he is thirsty, give him something to drink,
In doing this, you will heap burning coals on his head.'

[21]Do not be overcome by evil, but overcome evil with good.

Wrath and vengeance are not options for us. Why? Verse 19 tells us: because when we take vengeance, we are taking the place of God. 'Do not take revenge ... but leave room for God's wrath.' In verse 21, evil is to be overcome with good. It is not only a matter of not taking revenge, but a matter of doing positive good. And in this way – compare verse 20 – we will be heaping burning coals on the head of the person who has wronged us. That is, they will be ashamed because in the light of such goodness and goodwill, they are being antagonistic, which will shame them. Rather than taking revenge, we are to entrust ourselves to God.

What will God do? Paul explains this principle in Romans Chapter 13.

[1]Everyone must submit himself to the governing authorities, for there is no authority except that which God has established. The authorities that exist have been established by God. [2]Consequently, he who rebels against the authority is rebelling against what God has instituted, and those who do so will bring judgment on themselves. [3]For rulers hold no terror for those who do right, but for those who do wrong. Do you want to be free from fear of the one in authority? Then do what is right and he will commend you. [4]For he is God's servant to do you good. But if you do wrong, be afraid, for he does not bear the sword for nothing. He is God's servant, an agent of wrath to bring punishment on the wrongdoer.

God will often use the State as the instrument of punishment. Notice what Paul says in verse 1. God has established the authority of the state. Then in verse 2, he says the authority has been instituted by God: '... what God has instituted'. And he says in verse 4, that our ruler – the ruler of the State – is God's servant to do us good. On this basis, Paul could appeal to the Roman judicial system without breaching what the Lord Jesus was saying.[3] The State is the instrument which God mostly uses. So it is quite appropriate for a Christian, as part of an instrumentality of the State, to be a soldier, or a judge, or a policeman or policewoman, and to defend society against evil. But on a personal level, it is almost as though we are to be non-reactive. So, chapter 12 of Romans talks about our private responses, and chapter 13 about public responses.

Recently I was talking to the father of a young woman who was brutally raped and bludgeoned to death. He is a Christian man, and was telling me that many years later his pain continues to be very real. After their conviction, the judge recommended that the perpetrators should never be released. I asked the father about his attitude to these men who committed such animal barbarism. He said, 'They are where they should be, I have left them to the State.' He continued, 'I saw that the State was the instrument that God would use, so I have left them to the judgment of the State.' Now, that is an appropriate response. Our society has ensured that justice was carried out. As I spoke to this father, I could find no personal vindictiveness. He continues to pray for these men every day.

In Matthew chapter 5, verses 38-42, the Lord Jesus gives us four examples of how we are to resist evil.

The first example:

'If someone strikes you on the right cheek...'

In the Middle East, to be struck on the cheek was tantamount to a personal insult – challenging you to a duel to the death. Jesus says that in such a situation we are to respond with the poise

[3] Acts 25:8-12

of faith. Don't strike back as you probably want to do; rather, turn to him the other cheek. At this point of vulnerability, Jesus is saying, 'Don't respond. Allow the personal insults to go unanswered, the duel unaccepted.' Now, when I read this passage I tend to want to raise exceptions immediately. But Jesus does not allow me any exceptions. 'Blessed are the meek,' he says in chapter 5, verse 5.

The second example:
Someone comes along (v. 40), sues me and wants my tunic (which presumably was the undergarment). I give him the outer and top coat as well. I leave myself naked, even though it seems so unfair. In this verse we see Jesus' comments moving now from personal insult to possessions. He says we are to have an attitude of poise about our possessions as well. I find myself wanting to limit this. Surely there are occasions when I should not allow this to happen. But Jesus does not limit it. 'Be generous,' he says. And that requires trust. Notice verse 3: 'Blessed are the poor in spirit, for theirs is the kingdom of heaven.' So now I must detach myself from my rights, and from my things. Why?

There is an old proverb, 'Eagles don't catch flies.' Eagles are such majestic creatures, that they are looking for much bigger prey. We are not to be looking to get back at people, we are not to be people-destroyers, and we are not to be striving to get even. We are rather to be kingdom-builders, and we should be seeking people for the kingdom. An insult is very often an invitation to mission. Trouble is an opportunity to show ourselves as God's children. Being victimised gives us opportunities to show the surprising culture of the kingdom to which we belong. There is a bigger goal than our desire to get even.

The third example:
Jesus says (v. 41), 'If someone forces you to go one mile, go with him two miles.'

The Roman occupying army could force Jewish citizens, as they were walking along the road, to carry their military hardware – Roman military baggage, which would often be used within Palestine to put down a Jewish revolt. That is, they could be forced to carry military equipment that was going to kill their own people. Jesus is saying, 'If they ask you to go one mile, go two miles with them.' Again, I want to raise exceptions at this point; but Jesus doesn't. Be generous in your response, he says, and not self-defensive. Retaliation is out. The way of Christian maturity and poise comes from trusting God. Jesus is clear: 'Don't retaliate.'

And finally the fourth example:
Verse 42 is perhaps the hardest of all. 'Give to the one who asks you, and do not turn away from the one who wants to borrow from you.'

Someone borrows money from you – a common situation in life. But what if it results in a bad debt? In verse 42 we see the demonstration of godliness in the unspectacular situations in life. Just as the law in Deuteronomy 15 warns against being tight-fisted, Jesus says here, 'Be generous. Even if it affects your economic standing, show generosity.'

Again, Martin Luther, I think, reflects our view when he says this:

This word is too high. It is too hard for any of us to do. This is proved not merely by what Jesus says but by our own experience. You take any upright man or woman. They will get along very nicely with those who do not cut across them or provoke them. But let someone proffer only the slightest irritation and they will flare up in anger, if not against friends, then certainly against enemies. Flesh and blood cannot rise above natural retaliation.[4]

---

[4] Martin Luther, in R. Bainton, *Here I Stand: A Life of Martin Luther*, Abingdon-Cokesbury, 1950, p.46.

So here in Matthew 5:38-42 Jesus has provided us with four examples of maturity for the true citizen of His kingdom. However, we can live like this only if we acknowledge that we are blessed. 'Blessed are the poor.' 'Blessed are those who mourn.' 'Blessed are the meek.' 'Blessed are those who hunger.' 'Blessed are the merciful.' 'Blessed are the pure in heart.' 'Blessed are the peacemakers.' 'Blessed are those who are persecuted.' Luther was right. He said the only way you could 'detach' yourself from self-protection and self-justification is through the great doctrine of justification whereby God places you in Christ and sees you as you are in Christ.

The only way to be detached from myself is to realise that now I stand covered in the perfect righteousness of Christ. So if someone abuses me, if someone insults me, or slaps me, they are actually taking up arms against Christ Himself. So the poise of my response will come only from trusting in the indwelling Christ, who has covered me with His righteousness.

Revenge and anger are powerful emotions. We need to redirect these emotions into mission. We are not people-destroyers, we are people-builders. I am to see myself in Christ, for that is where my ultimate security lies.

I read an article about a person who had gone back to the secular workforce after years in Anglican ministry.[5] From his experience, he noticed very little verbal witnessing going on in the workplace. However, he said the powerful Christian witness is seen in the way Christians react to stressful situations. That in itself is a tantalizing thing: to see Christians respond in a way that is totally surprising. We must radically reject self-assertion in the face of injury to our honour and rights, unfair treatment, exploitation and our feelings of being taken advantage of.

'Christians are surprising people,' said theologian Dietrich Bonhoeffer. Jesus told His disciples to turn the other cheek, to give the extra coat, and to go the extra mile. In Victor Hugo's

---

[5] Andrew Reid, 'Reflections from a minister at work (Parts 1 and 2)', in *The Briefing*, Issues 265/6, December 2000, and Issue 267, February 2001 (Matthias Media).

Les Misérables, Jean Valjean is given hospitality in the bishop's house. He then steals the bishop's silver cutlery. The police catch him and take him back to the bishop's house. How does the bishop respond? In a most surprising way. 'My man, why didn't you take the candlesticks as well? Here they are, take them!' Jean Valjean realises that the bishop has bought him back for God. It's such a surprising response from the bishop, isn't it?

Someone cuts in on you in the traffic. Someone in the workplace takes advantage of you. Someone slacks off in their duties and the burden falls to you. You are on the bus, or on the train, and someone pushes into the best seat. You are queuing at the sports event and someone gets in front of you for a better seat. Once I was waiting with my bags at the airport, and as I turned around the man behind me jumped in front of me in the queue. How dare he! The surprising response would be, 'Can I help you with your bags?'

If you are in public office, seek justice. If you are acting privately, seek peace. We must walk in humility, in a way that is willing to lose face, with bravery but not needing to appear brave. If we do nothing, it does not mean we are cowards; it may mean we are showing the essence of courage.

I remember listening to a debate in Federal Parliament between the Australian Prime Minister and the Leader of the Opposition, who had just sacked one of his Shadow Cabinet Ministers. The Prime Minister gave a majestic speech. He said the Leader of the Opposition had the failing of all those who are really weak – they need to prove their strength. He said that by sacking this Shadow Minister, he was really showing that he was inherently weak.

We think we have things to prove, we have to strike back, we must even things up. But the reality of the way of Christ, the way of maturity, is that we will not strike back. 'Here, take the candlesticks as well.'

In Michael Leunig's wonderful cartoon, *The Club*, a little man is standing there when a finger comes down from above. A voice says, 'Come to the Club', and the man is filled with fear.

'The Club?' he says.

'Yes, you're being ushered to the Club.'

'Isn't the Club just for a few?'

'No, you come to the Club.'

He goes to the Club, and looks around. Every single person in the human race is there. This is not a gathering of some elite group; this is a gathering of everyone. On the wall he sees the motto in this Human Club: 'Everything is funny [that is, peculiar]. Growth comes through humiliation. Wisdom comes through loss.'

Jesus is talking about humiliating circumstances. He is talking about circumstances in which you may lose the money you lend. That is kingdom culture. 'Growth comes through humiliation. Wisdom comes through loss.' The radical strength of not getting back at someone, the radical strength required to detach yourself from your own rights, is true strength.

Let's review another Bible reference. 1 Corinthians chapter 6, verse 7:

> The very fact that you have lawsuits among you means that you have been completely defeated already. Why not rather be wronged? Why not rather be cheated?

We need to pray that the Lord would deliver us from being involved in any kind of retaliation. 'Eagles don't catch flies.' Pray that we will have the poise that comes from detachment from self. Pray that we will be generous, and that in our generosity (a surprising response), we will show forth a very real trust in God.

Listen to these words spoken about a man:

House bombed; living day by day for thirteen years under constant threats of death; maliciously accused of being a Communist; falsely accused of being insincere ...; stabbed by a member of his own race; slugged in a hotel lobby; jailed over twenty times; occasionally deeply hurt because friends betrayed him – and yet this man had no bitterness in his heart, no rancour in his soul, no revenge in his mind; and he went up and down the length and breadth of this world preaching non-violence and the redemptive power of love.[6]

The words were spoken at the funeral of that man. Martin Luther King had just been assassinated, and these were the words that marked him out: 'Non-violence and the redemptive power of love.' The apostle Peter said, 'To this you were called,' – that is, being persecuted though innocent – 'because Christ suffered for you, leaving you an example that you should follow in his steps.'[7]

The Lord Jesus said, 'If someone slaps you on one cheek, turn to him the other. If someone wants to sue you for one item of clothing, give him the others as well. If someone wants to push you into their service and slavery for a while, go. Be surprising people. Give to the one who asks you and do not turn away from the one who wants to borrow from you.' What did Jeremiah say to the Jews who were going to be enslaved in the exile? He said, 'You're going into slavery. Be very good slaves![8] Surprise them. Draw from them the testimony, "We've never had such good slaves as this!"'

That is the culture of God's kingdom.

---

6 C. S. King, quoting Dr Benjamin Mays, *My Life with Martin Luther King Jr.*, London: Hodder and Stoughton, 1970, p 365-369.

7 1 Peter 2:21

8 See Jeremiah 29.

CHAPTER THREE

NOTHING BUT MAMMALS

MATTHEW 5:27-30

In Matthew, chapter 5, verses 27-30, our Lord Jesus says:

> [27]You have heard that it was said, 'Do not commit adultery.'
> [28]But I tell you that anyone who looks at a woman lustfully
> has already committed adultery with her in his heart. [29]If
> your right eye causes you to sin, gouge it out and throw it
> away. It is better for you to lose one part of your body than
> for your whole body to be thrown into hell. [30]And if your
> right hand causes you to sin, cut it off and throw it away. It
> is better for you to lose one part of your body than for your
> whole body to go into hell.

You may have heard these song words from the rock band the
Bloodhound Gang:

> You and me baby ain't nothin' but mammals,
> So let's do it like they do on the Discovery Channel.[1]

I can remember these words after hearing them only twice,
so I gather that kids in your youth group – and maybe you –

---

[1] Bloodhound Gang, 'The Bad Touch', from the album *Hooray for Boobies*, Interscope
Records, 2000.

have memorised the whole song, and may be tempted to live according to the lyrics of that song.

At the Katoomba Men's Convention, when there are 3,000 men in the auditorium, there is usually soft background noise: seats creaking, and people moving and turning pages in Bibles. What transforms soft noise into pin-dropping silence at a Men's Convention is when one of the speakers takes some exegetical point from the Bible and actually applies it to the sex lives of the men there. The men sit up and pay attention, because they know this is an area where they need help. Our silence on these issues relating to sex and adultery is a guilty silence.

Let's begin by revisiting what the Bible has to say about sex and marriage. In Ephesians, chapter 5, verse 31, you will notice that, for the fourth time in Scripture, we have what has been called God's blueprint for marriage. Paul, inspired by the Spirit, now repeats the words that first appear in Genesis 2:24:

> [31]For this reason a man will leave his father and mother and be united to his wife, and the two will become one flesh.

You will remember that, according to Genesis, woman was made to be man's companion. Here Paul quotes again the ground rules for the relationship.

Firstly, a man will leave his father and mother. Normally in that society a man would take his wife back to live in his father's house, and yet they must form a distinctive household. The priority for the man is no longer his relationship to his parents. His principal responsibility is now the relationship to his wife. It is his responsibility to place all his former family relationships one step back.

Secondly, the man and woman must be united to one another. Literally this means they must be 'glued' to one another. This is to be a lifelong commitment. It is not something they just do on a whim, or commit themselves to for only a limited time.

Thirdly, '... and the two will become one flesh'. They will become an intimate union, which includes sexual intimacy.

Jews believe this. Christians believe this as well. What Christians uniquely believe, which Jews do not believe, is verse 32:

> This is a profound mystery – but I am talking about Christ
> and the church.

This is what we uniquely believe about marriage – that marriage points away from itself to a greater reality, and in that sense is sacramental. The relationship of a husband and wife is to be a visual aid for the relationship of Jesus and His church. The husband is to love his wife as Jesus loves the church. The wife is to submit to and honour the leadership of her husband as the church does to the Lord Jesus.

Notice that this leaving, and cleaving, and one flesh, are to be taken together. Sex, of course, can be mishandled. In this sense, sex is like petrol. You can siphon petrol out of your car, put it into a saucer and sniff it, and it will destroy your brain. Or if you throw petrol on your barbecue, you will lose your barbecue. But if you put petrol into the car, in the environment for which it was intended, it will get you from A to B. It is very good in that environment.

Notice also that God says from the very beginning, from Genesis, chapter 2, that the environment for sex, for becoming one, is an environment of a lifelong, covenantal commitment, of leaving and of being united to another. That is God's intended environment for sexual expression. Sex is unique body language. It is allowing your body to say, 'I am committed to you for life.' But sex, if it occurs apart from this lifelong, covenantal relationship, is allowing your body to tell a lie, because it is allowing your body to say something that you are not prepared to say. Those who say that sex is just a matter of moving body parts do not really understand it. It is a bonding experience, and so it is a terrible thing when someone is used sexually and discarded. So much hurt is done and anger created when someone is simply discarded. There is no contraceptive for a broken heart. Those who have been victimised and abused know more than others what a destructive thing sex can be when it is taken out of its God-ordained environment.

Now, whether at this moment you are married or you are single, it is for your good that the Lord Jesus speaks. In Matthew, chapter 5, verse 20, Jesus tells His disciples, 'Unless your righteousness surpasses that of the Pharisees and the teachers of the law, you will certainly not enter the kingdom of heaven.'

How can our righteousness surpass theirs? He gives us the first example in verse 21 when He says, 'You have heard that it was said, "Don't murder", but you see that the act of murder has behind it an attitude of anger.' Therefore Jesus is saying that in the kingdom of God, righteousness extends beyond the act, to the thought.

Jesus' second example concerns adultery. Notice that in verses 27-28 Jesus repeats the pattern, 'You have heard that it was said ... but I tell you ...' It would be crazy if I were to say something like, 'You've heard that the Bible says ... but I'm telling you this ...' Jesus is putting His word on a par with the word of Scripture. In verse 27 he quotes the seventh commandment when he says, 'You have heard that it was said, "Do not commit adultery".' Literally this means do not have sexual relations with anyone with whom you are not in this lifelong, covenant commitment of marriage. To be having sex outside of that relationship is adultery. Within the scheme of the Ten Commandments, this is number seven. It is in the area of loving your neighbour, as expressed in commandments five through to ten, and this one involves respecting your neighbour's body.

Jesus does not set the commandment aside; he just takes it to the level of attitude. Adultery, he says, goes beyond the act to the thought. Verse 28 says, 'I tell you that anyone who looks at a woman lustfully has already committed adultery with her in his heart.' This is shocking teaching! It shocks us that adultery in the mind is still adultery! He puts physical and mental adultery on the same level.

What does this lustful look mean? It is the same word in Greek as the word that is translated 'covet' in the Ten Commandments. It is the look of 'I would if I could'. It is the look with the purpose that 'this woman is here to bring me satisfaction'. In the Greek the verb is in the present continuous tense, so it is referring to whoever looks at a woman in this continuing way. It is not just a glance. It is more of a gaze. It is a leer. Jesus says, and we know ourselves, that it comes quite naturally to us. As our car goes from first to fifth gear, we can easily go from admiration, to desire, to adultery – if not physically, then adultery in the mind. It is automatic transmission.

You know what it can be like. You flip over a page in a magazine and you come upon an image, and you know that this is no place for a believer's eyes, but you linger. You have the TV remote control and you change channels, and you know this is no place for a believer to be. You are in enemy-occupied territory. Adultery has an anatomy, it has a structure, it has a skeleton, it has a progression.

King David is probably the best example of this. There he is on the roof of his palace while his men are off in battle. He is glancing around the city. And his glance turns to a gaze. He settles into automatic. His passion shifts gear into adultery when he sees the beautiful Bathsheba. This is how Scripture reports the event – he sent for her, she came, he slept with her, she returned home – all very black and white.[2] It started with a glance, which, unchecked, turned into a gaze, which, unchecked, went from admiration to desire to adultery. So did he get away with it? A one-night stand, no complications? No. The prophet Nathan knew he had to confront his own king, who had the power to put him to death, so he had to choose his words very well. King David had been a shepherd, so Nathan told him a shepherdly story. It was a story about a family with one little sheep that was just like a member of the family, a pet; and about a rich man, who had many sheep. This rich man had a friend come for dinner. Instead

---

[2] See 2 Samuel 11

of barbecuing one of the many sheep from his flock, he took this one little lamb that belonged to the neighbouring family. King David responds, 'The man should die!' And Nathan says, 'You are that man! You took Bathsheba into your own bed.'[3]

David had to learn that there is nothing done in secret. God is the One to whom all desires are known and from whom no secrets are hidden. Here is an example for us in Scripture, if we need this sort of encouragement: that although temptation is so appealing, it does not pay dividends. I put it to you that if you were looking to invest money in a company, you would never choose the Temptation Company, would you? Its prospectus may look good, and glossy, and terrific. All the desire is there. But the company never pays the dividends it promises.

I remember one night when I had to go to pick up one of our children from a school dance held at a Sydney hotel in Kings Cross. I had to be there at midnight. 'Dad', I was told, 'don't come early. I don't want them to see you. Stay in the car, I don't want you to come inside.' So I was driving up this street on a Saturday night at about a quarter to twelve. As you drive along the street, you look at the footpath, and every form of body is on sale there. It all looks very attractive. It's like a smorgasbord: just stop, open the car door, take your pick and away you go. And wouldn't the devil be happy! No strings attached! What did Nathan say to his king? 'You have made the enemies of the Lord show utter contempt for the Lord.'[4] If you opened the door and invited temptation in, the devil would be laughing, 'You, a Christian, doing this!' Nathan was right: David's actions had caused God's enemies to show him contempt. Temptation makes big promises, but it never fulfils. It never delivers.

What a hard saying this is. In Matthew chapter 5, verse 3, we find a saying that reminds us of our own poverty of spirit. It comes naturally to us to look lustfully, and so this verse reminds us that we are 'poor in spirit' and we need help. Chapter 5, verse 8,

---

[3] 2 Samuel 12:1-7
[4] 2 Samuel 12:14

says, 'Blessed are the pure in heart, for they will see God.' In so many ways we are not pure, so this verse drives us back to our dependence on God. Martin Luther said, 'If no other work were commanded but chastity alone, we would all have enough to do with this one ... In this work a good strong faith is a great help, more noticeably so than in any other.'[5] Lord God, I am so weak, I am so impure, please help me.

Jesus tells us what we are to do about that, in verses 29 and 30.

> [29]If your right eye causes you to sin, gouge it out and throw it away. It is better for you to lose one part of your body than for your whole body to be thrown into hell. [30]And if your right hand causes you to sin, cut if off and throw it away. It is better for you to lose one part of your body than for your whole body to go into hell.

Jesus uses, I believe, exaggerated language here. But it gets the point across – this requires swift, radical action. Did you know that Jesus, in Matthew's Gospel, mentions the place of Gehenna seven times, and twice in these two verses? Gehenna is translated in the NIV, in verses 29 and 30, as 'hell'. But it is literally 'Gehenna', a valley outside of Jerusalem, a place where child sacrifices once had been made to pagan gods. It always had the stench and status of that sort of a place. But in the days of Jesus, Gehenna was the garbage dump of the city. It was a smouldering place of garbage. And it becomes, therefore, according to the Lord Jesus, a fitting picture of the smouldering garbage dump of hell itself. It is a place to be avoided.

We need to take radical action: that is what Jesus is saying. In verse 29 he says, 'If your right eye (that is, your best eye) causes you to sin, gouge it out and throw it away.' Why do I believe that this is exaggerated language? Because, if you have only got one eye, it does not make you less lustful. 'If your right hand causes

---

[5] M. Luther, *A Treatise on Good Works: The 6th (7th) Commandment*, text available at http://www.ccel.org/ccel/luther/good_works.ix.html

you to sin, (your best hand) cut it off.' Yet if you cut your right hand off, it doesn't make you a less lustful person. Lust comes from inside. Origen was the great father of the allegorical, the spiritual, method of biblical interpretation; and he took these verses quite literally. He proposed that under every literal interpretation of Scripture there was a deeper meaning of the text. Yet when he read Matthew's Gospel which said some men had been made eunuchs for the sake of the kingdom of heaven, wouldn't you think he would interpret that one spiritually, or allegorically? But he didn't! He interpreted it literally! He had himself made a eunuch for the sake of the kingdom of God. Eusebius, the church historian, said that although that showed Origen's great continence and self-control, it was an absurd interpretation of the text.[6]

Remarkably, there have been people who have actually gouged out their right eye. Some people have cut off their right hand. You will find, of course, that it does not help you in this matter of lust. It is appropriate that you do something with your eye because it is through the eye that lust comes. Notice that the seventh commandment, which prohibits adultery, belongs in the context of all Ten commandments. The Ten Commandments begin with your recognition of God. What then does lust and spiritual adultery mean? It is a lack of trust in God to provide for your needs. It results in taking things into your own hands. It is a lack of trust in God to provide for your needs in His way and in His time. This lustful look also reflects a wrong view of people, that they are commodities to be used and discarded by the one who lusts.

What are we to be doing? In Matthew, chapter 5, verse 6, the Lord Jesus says we are to hunger and thirst for righteousness. That is what we are to covet, that is literally what we are to lust for. We are to lust for righteousness, not for another person's body to use in an illegitimate way.

---

[6] Eusebius, *The Church History*, Penguin Books, Harmondsworth, 1965, p 247.

Jesus makes it clear to the disciples that this requires careful, determined action. We are always being observed. As a member of God's kingdom, be very careful. Jesus says to take action. It is better to suffer the small loss of instant gratification now, than to suffer the ultimate loss later and end up in Gehenna itself, in the place of hell.

Let me apply this teaching. I want to point out a number of things.

First of all, this commandment of Jesus is a good one, because it reminds us how frail we are; and we need warnings like this. In Proverbs, chapters 6 and 7, Solomon gives these sorts of warnings to his son. I don't know who the son of Solomon was, but he was probably an adolescent, which is why the early chapters of Proverbs are great chapters to be reading to your adolescent children. The burden of Proverbs, chapters 1–9, is like a response to the question, 'Is there one thing you would like to say to adolescents today, Solomon?' He says, 'Yes, too right. I'd like to tell them to listen to their parents.' That is what he says. Look through Proverbs 1–9 and see how often he says, 'Listen, my son, listen to a father's instruction! Listen, my son! Listen to a mother! She loves you!' What is the last thing adolescents want to do? They never want to listen. Solomon is saying, 'Listen! Listen! Listen!'

In Proverbs, chapter 6, verse 27, the writer talks about adultery and he says, 'Can a man scoop fire into his lap?' Imagine the coals of a barbecue. Someone, as a party trick says, 'Let's tip the hot coals into his lap!' Now, what are you going to do? You are going to get out of there quickly, because if they scoop fire into your lap your clothes are going to be burned. And probably a lot more, too!

> [28]Can a man walk on hot coals without his feet being scorched?
> [29]So is he who sleeps with another man's wife;
> no-one who touches her will go unpunished.

Solomon uses vivid pictures to get the meaning across.

Then in Proverbs, chapter 7, verse 22-27, the young man sees the prostitute and goes with her.

> 22All at once he followed her
>   like an ox going to the slaughter,
> Like a deer stepping into a noose
>   23till an arrow pierces his liver,
> like a bird darting into a snare,
>   little knowing it will cost him his life.
> 24Now then, my sons, listen to me;
>   Pay attention to what I say.
> 25Do not let your heart turn to her ways
>   or stray into her paths.
> 26Many are the victims she has brought down;
>   Her slain are a mighty throng.
> 27Her house is a highway to the grave,
>   leading down to the chambers of death.

We need to hear these words. We need these sorts of reminders.

Secondly, notice that these words of our Lord Jesus are for the protection of our ongoing purity. These words drive us home when we should be home and not out on the streets. When we go into the newsagent's to get Saturday's *Herald*, these words drive us straight out again, without lingering to look at other magazines. These words cause us to take our own book to the doctor's surgery because we do not want to read the 'junk' in the waiting room there. These words drive us to be very careful of late night-television. These words drive us to be very careful about what we go and fill our minds with at the movies or from the video store.

What a foolish thing it is to have an overdeveloped sense of trust in yourself. Jesus says, 'Adultery in the mind is adultery.' The young man goes to his old pastor and asks, 'When is it that

I'll cease to be afflicted by the temptations of the flesh?' The pastor wisely, from all his experience, says, 'I wouldn't trust myself until I've been dead three days!' It is when you are young that you have an overdeveloped confidence in your own ability to take everything that comes flashing to you – in music clips, on DVDs, at the movies – and your ability not to be affected by it. It is foolish immaturity, because our Lord Jesus says, 'Adultery in the mind is adultery.' So be very careful, for, while it may appear attractive, it destroys relationships – it pays no meaningful dividend.

Thirdly, this saying of Jesus is protective of women. What a dreadful thing it is to be constantly the subject of a gaze, a leer, as though you are just an object. So this is protective of the humanity of women. They are not objects to be leered at.

Fourthly, notice that in Matthew 5, verse 28, the man who is actually looking at the woman lustfully is responsible for his actions. What I am about to say does not relieve the man of the responsibility not to look lustfully at women. However, could I say to women, please don't dress in such a way that tantalises, that draws out the look. Don't dress in such a way that makes it hard for your brother. Rather, help him to lust after righteousness and not after a woman. And at this point I feel I should also urge women to resist our culture. At so many points we must be cultural atheists. Resist the way fashion pushes you. For the sake of your brothers, I plead with you, dress and act in a way that is not tantalising. Act in such a way as helps us, because we are responsible. I am not trying to shift responsibility, but we do need to be considerate of one another in the way we act, in the way we dress and in the way we speak, because Jesus says, 'Adultery in the mind is adultery.' And in the same way as the Song of Songs addresses the 'Daughters of Jerusalem' men likewise need to be aware of clothing, and to make sure that in relationships they 'do not arouse or awaken love until it so desires'.[7]

Now, finally, David says in Psalm 119, verse 9:

> How can a young man keep his way pure?
>   By living according to your word.

What a great verse that is! Remember, we are to hunger and thirst after righteousness. Resist the easy acceptance of adultery. This is what the Heidelberg Catechism says:

> What is God's will for us in the seventh commandment? God condemns all unchastity in the seventh commandment, and we should detest it and, married or single, live decent and chaste lives.[8]

Ask yourself the following questions: Is adultery and lust a delight which you enjoy? Is it something that is just part of your normal everyday life? Is it something that you enjoy, or is it something that is a burden to be avoided? For the believer, for the true citizen of God's kingdom, it will be a burden. It will remind us again of our frailty. It will drive us back to acknowledging our poverty in spirit and we will cry out to God for mercy; that we would covet righteousness, hunger and thirst for righteousness and trust Him to fulfil our needs.

The Lord Jesus here shows his great respect for marriage, and he protects marriage by urging the avoidance of adultery at all costs.

You can be absolutely sure that the devil is able to take these words and accuse you about your past, because your past is full of these sorts of mistakes. The devil is the accuser. But the Holy Spirit has nothing to do with accusation. The Holy Spirit convicts. The Holy Spirit does not take you back to your past;

---

[7] Song of Songs 2:7
[8] Question 108, *The Heidelberg Catechism*, CRC Publications, Grand Rapids, 1989, p. 151.

He takes you away from your past and He drives you to Jesus, because it is there that you will find forgiveness and there that you will find the Holy Spirit. So do not let the devil accuse you in relation to these words. Ask that the Holy Spirit will convict you and drive you to Jesus for cleansing, and that you might have the fullness of his Spirit so that you can live consistently with what our Lord Jesus says.

At a recent Katoomba Christian Convention, one of the speakers, who was from a Buddhist background, gave his testimony of how he became a Christian. He said it started when he was walking along the beach with a friend of his from university. He asked his friend, 'What does it mean to be a Christian?' His friend simply answered: 'It means that I have lost control of my life to Jesus.'

Have you lost control of your life; your activities, your thought life, your looking, your gazing? Have you lost control of your life to Jesus?

CHAPTER FOUR

UNFORGIVENESS

MATTHEW 6:12-15

At the end of Year 10, our son came home from school with a report from his drama teacher which said, 'It seems that your son was born in a drama theatre rather than a hospital theatre.' He was born for the stage. So, in preparation and review for his exams, he and I together were going through the subject 'Drama', which he was taking as one of his senior subjects. I learned with him to look for reversals in a script, to look for and recognise sub-plots in the script, character development, and the major movements in the drama. And so, inspired by that, I have written a three-act drama by way of introduction.

Act One
A man has overspent his credit card. He has debts of $20,000, which he cannot repay. His salary cannot even keep up with the interest payments. The bank can bankrupt him by selling his mortgaged home. The man goes to his bank manager and begs for leniency. The bank manager miraculously wipes the debt off. (Now that is a story you do not hear often. Remember, this is fiction!) Relief and joy are now the dominating emotions.

Whereas before we had sorrow for this man because of his great need, now we are filled with feelings of relief for him, and even feelings of goodwill towards the bank! We do not often have those sorts of feelings for banks, but now we do.

Act Two

The man leaves the bank and runs into an acquaintance in the street. He remembers that he did a job for this man a couple of months ago and the man owes him $1,000. He demands payment. He has no patience. 'I am going to begin proceedings against you immediately,' he tells the debtor. Now our feelings are revulsion for this man and sorrow for his debtor. You see, in Act One, mercy triumphed, and we felt right about that. In Act Two, justice triumphs, and that builds up stress. What is going to happen next?

Act Three

The bank manager hears what has happened. He brings the man back in and tells him that he will prosecute him for his debt. Even though the bank manager had been merciful, now, because of this man's lack of mercy, the manager will see that justice is done.

You will recognise that this script is not original. Jesus, Himself, is the playwright. It is our Father in heaven who is the bank manager, who loves mercy, and will treat us with justice unless we treat others mercifully. You can read the original script later on in Matthew's Gospel.[1]

Here is another case study. Have you ever wondered why the Lord Jesus loved Samaritans? Samaritans were a mongrel race: they were half Jew and half Gentile. They were despised. In the minds of the Jews, they were like tax collectors and sinners. Yet the Lord Jesus seems to go out of His way, in John

---

[1] See Matthew 18:21-35.

4, to travel through Samaritan territory so that He can reach the woman of Samaria; and, as a result, many Samaritans come to the conviction that Jesus is the Saviour of the world. In Luke chapter 10, Jesus tells a story about Samaritans, putting them in a good light. He tells the story about the 'Good Samaritan' who, unlike many Jews of the time, loves without concern for colour, race or creed. In Acts, chapter 1, verse 8, in Jesus' last recorded words before His ascension, He remembers the Samaritans: the gospel will go from Jerusalem to Judea, to Samaria.

Why does Jesus have this special relationship with the Samaritans? Do they deserve it? If that is the case, it is only justice. But no, it is contrary to their deserving. We read in Luke, chapter 9, that when Jesus comes to a Samaritan village, the Samaritans reject Him. The disciples, James and John, come and say to Jesus, 'Shall we call down fire from heaven and burn these Samaritans up?' That would be just, but Jesus rebukes them because He loves mercy. You see, the Lord Jesus, in the case of the Samaritans, will see that mercy triumphs over justice because He is the God who does not treat us as our sins deserve.

James, chapter 2, verses 12 and 13, says:

> [12]Speak and act as those who are going to be judged by the law that gives freedom, [13]because judgment without mercy will be shown to anyone who has not been merciful. Mercy triumphs over judgment.

You see, God loves mercy. And God will see that mercy triumphs, except in the case of the person who insists that their own personal justice should triumph. In that case, God will treat them as they have treated others, not with mercy, but He will be guided by justice. It is a very great challenge to us.

This brings us back to Matthew, chapter 6. There are times when we will duck and weave away from truths that rip towards us, in the same way that in cricket a batsman ducks to avoid a Glenn McGrath bumper.[2] You may well have claimed on the question of loving your enemies, 'I've got no enemies.' Do not believe yourself. That is ducking out of the way of a bumper! You *have* got people you find hard to love. You might have thought of all sorts of exceptions to turning the other cheek. That is ducking the bumper! Jesus provides no exceptions for us.

In Matthew, chapter 6, Jesus says it is all about our motivation. He is teaching about prayer and in verse 5 He says, 'When you pray, don't be like the hypocrites. They love to pray standing up, to be seen by people.' Then in verse 7, 'And when you pray, don't keep babbling like the pagans, because they think that they will be heard for the flood of their words.' They believe that they can manipulate their god using their beads or mantras, or simply by the volume of their words. Don't be like them, he warns. In verses 9-13 Jesus says, 'This is how you are to pray ...' This is where Jesus teaches about God and about ourselves. Notice the sheer economy of words:

> Our Father in heaven,
> Hallowed be your name,
> [10]Your kingdom come,
> Your will be done
>   On earth as it is in heaven.

The first part shows that we can address God as our Father. Then we see that the chief concern of the citizen of the kingdom is the honour of God's reputation: the weight of His name, His glory, the establishment of His rule, His kingdom on earth. The concern is that God's kingdom be established in all places, including wherever we are now. That is our great concern.

---

[2] In Australian cricket, a 'bumper' is a pitched ball that hits the ground and then bounces up near the batter's head or shoulders; it is therefore akin to the 'beanball' in American baseball.

But we have needs as well. Very practically, verse 11 says, 'Give us today our daily bread.' We need food because we have a body. But we are more than just body. We need spiritual help.

> [12]Forgive us our debts,
>   As we also have forgiven our debtors,
> [13]And lead us not into temptation,
> But deliver us from the evil one.

Notice how the Lord Jesus, in verses 14 and 15 below, could have summed up by repeating any of those requests to God in verses 9-13; but He simply repeats the one in verse 12, as though that is the one that will most shock His listeners, and needs exposition.

> [14]For if you forgive men when they sin against you, your heavenly Father will also forgive you. [15]But if you do not forgive men their sins, your Father will not forgive your sins.

So, it's on this twelfth verse that I want to focus: on what Augustine called 'the terrible petition'.[3] 'Forgive us our debts' is a Hebrew way of talking about sins. Luke says, 'Forgive us our sins.' But Matthew says, 'Forgive us our debts as we have forgiven our debtors.'

There are four questions about forgiveness that need answering.

First: Why do believers need to ask for ongoing forgiveness if we are already right with God in Christ? If we are justified – if God has made us right with Himself on the basis of the death of His son Jesus – why do we need to go on asking for forgiveness?

The reason, of course, is because we go on being sinful. We go on committing sins, offensive to God and offensive to others. King David reminds us that all sin has two dimensions – it is

---

[3] Augustine *Enchiridion: On Faith, Hope, and Love,* Chapter 21

against people and it is against God. But David, after his sin with Bathsheba (which involved adultery and murder, two very human-centred sins), says, 'Against you, you only, have I sinned and done what is evil in your sight.'[4] So Jesus says we are to seek forgiveness because we are sinful, and then make restitution with others.

You see, there are certain things we cannot do for ourselves. You may remember the TV show, *Gilligan's Island*. The castaways on Gilligan's Island could do just about anything. They could build roads, they could build homes with modern conveniences. The only thing they could not do was get off the island. We, too, can do so much. Look at our technological advances, our knowledge explosion, our communications and our medical advances. But there is one thing none of us can do. We cannot forgive ourselves. We need God to forgive us, and that is why we need to pray that God *will* forgive us.

The second question: Is my forgiveness of others really the basis of God's forgiveness of me?

No. The basis of God's forgiveness of you is the work of Jesus. But there is an important condition in verse 12: 'Forgive me my debts – forgive us our debts – as we also have forgiven our debtors.' Many will not pray that second line – or if we do pray it, we do not actually mean it – that God will be as merciful to me as I am to others, that He will treat me as a sinner in exactly the same way as I treat others who have offended me.

Now, we have already seen in the first drama which began this chapter, how incongruous, how contradictory, how incompatible it is to be forgiven much and yet not to forgive. The reality of my forgiveness must show itself in my forgiveness of others. That is what makes Act Two so deplorable, that the man, over a trifling issue, treated the other person so contrary to his own treatment. Consider again what God says in James, chapter 2, verse 13: 'I

---

[4] Psalm 51:4

will not allow justice to triumph over mercy – except in the case of the person who *does* allow justice to triumph over mercy.'

We need to keep this in mind because we do not heed it. (The Lord Jesus knows about pain. He knows about hurt. He knows about all these things.) This is a very dangerous prayer, because if you pray this prayer and still determine to go on being unforgiving and bearing grudges, then God will be true to His Word. If I were to say, 'People will go to hell if they don't trust in the Lord Jesus,' I think you would say, 'I agree with that.' However, if I were to say, 'People will go to hell unless they get rid of their unforgiving spirits,' you might question that. But the reality of these petitions is exactly that. Without forgiveness, I cannot see the face of God. He will see that mercy triumphs over judgment through His Son. But if I go on bearing grudges and seeing judgment triumph, I am praying against myself, because mercy must flow from the reception of mercy. If I am forgiven, I will forgive. That is why Augustine called this 'the terrible petition', for we are asking God to apply to us the same mercy as we offer to those who sin against us.

I remember a friend telling the story some years ago about driving home from church on a rainy Sunday night. He had come to a stop at a red light. There were no other cars immediately behind him, but as he looked in the rear mirror, he could see a car in the distance. As he watched, it kept coming, and coming, until it slammed straight into the back of his car. My friend was angry. He got out of his car and said to the other driver, 'Are you blind or something? I'm the only car on the road and you've run straight into the back of me.'

The driver got out and said, 'Oh yeah, yeah.'

It was clear he was a very young driver, and inexperienced.

'So I suppose you haven't got your licence with you?"

'No, I haven't.'

'You've stolen this car, have you?'

'No, I haven't stolen the car.'

'Oh come on, you're too young to own this! Who would give you a car like this?'

'My next-door neighbour gave it to me so I could impress a girl. Please don't put me in. Please don't turn me in.'

And my friend said, 'If I don't turn you in, it's going to cost me a lot of money to get this car fixed. But because God has been merciful to me, I won't turn you in. But it's going to cost me. Just as God's forgiveness of me cost Him, my forgiveness of you is going to cost me as well.'

And with that my friend got back into his car, and drove away.

That is a great model, isn't it? 'Forgive us as we forgive.' We might think that to forgive would make us look stupid, or unwise. But the Lord Jesus says, 'Forgive us as we forgive.' God will apply to us our own standards of mercy.

The third question: Why is it important to forgive?

The first reason why it is important to forgive is because, according to Time magazine, offering forgiveness is good for you.[5] It is therapeutic. About $10 million is being sunk into the National Association of Forgiveness because the American Psychological Association has discovered that there is great liberating power in forgiveness. If we want to reduce violence and increase psychological stability, we need to work on forgiveness rather than retaliation. Dr Robert Enright, Professor of Human Development at the University of Minnesota and author of several books on forgiveness, writes, 'Forgiveness is such a powerful experience that it can, under the right circumstances, heal you emotionally, help the one forgiven and even heal your relationships.'[6] So even the social sciences are saying it is good for us to forgive. The Lord Jesus also says it is good for us to forgive, but He adds that the most important thing is to be forgiven first, and then to forgive.

---

[5] D .Van Biema, 'Should All Be Forgiven?", *Time Magazine*, April 5, 1999.

[6] R. Enright, *Forgiveness is a Choice*, APA Books, 2001, p. 263.

The second reason we are to forgive is because God loves mercy, and we show we are His children by loving mercy. In the movie *Schindler's List,* the camp commandant was deciding whether or not he would kill the boy who could not clean the stain out of his bathtub. He was urged not to shoot the boy as he ran back to the camp because it would take more strength to forgive than to take retribution. You could see the battle going on in that man's mind, until he picked up the long-distance gun and killed the boy, simply because he hadn't been able to get a stain out of a bathtub. He reduced himself to the level of an animal: that is what we are doing when we kill. He could have been God-like, because that is what we are when we forgive. It means ensuring, as our heavenly Father does, that mercy triumphs over judgment.

The third reason to forgive is because the church is a community based on forgiveness. We could not know God apart from forgiveness. None of us could be in fellowship together if it were not for forgiveness. Because we are correspondingly hurting and offending one another, and being hurt and offended by one another, so we always need to be forgiving one another. Unforgiveness poisons us and our communities. In our pride we minimise our own sin and what our forgiveness cost God, and we maximise the sin against us. We justify being unforgiving. Imagine the chaos in our community if we were not able to forgive. And therefore, the Lord Jesus makes it clear that the Father will forgive us, so now we must go and show that we have been transformed by this gospel, and put our pride behind us by forgiving others who have sinned against us. The church is the community of God's forgiven and forgiving people.

The fourth question – the big question: How can I forgive?

It is very hard to forgive. It is very hard to forgive when people do the wrong thing by you, and it seems to me it is even harder to forgive when people do the wrong thing to those you love, your family members. But we must. Let me say three things.

Firstly, you must make this a matter of prayer, because we can so easily become grudging. You must put off any vestige of, or resemblance to, retribution and grudges. And then you must put on positive goodwill to the other. Put off grudge-bearing, remembering wrongs done. And put on total goodwill to the other person, because in this kingdom the citizen's concern is for forgiveness and mercy, and not for personal justice and retribution.

Secondly, be forgiving in surprising ways. When people do the wrong thing by you, come back with generosity of spirit: not only do the right thing, but do even more than the right thing. You cannot do that unless you come to the gospel of this kingdom and allow yourself to be changed by it. What a tragedy it is to find churches that are driven apart by unforgiveness, by people who pray the Lord's Prayer every week at least and are actually praying against themselves. They are really praying, 'Father forgive me my debts, but don't do it – because I am not willing to forgive the debts of others.' The two graces of mercy from God and mercy to others are inseparable. How shocked people will be when they are rejected from heaven because they have harboured an unforgiving spirit.

When the Nazis invaded Poland, one of the Jewish leaders of the Warsaw ghetto said, 'I cannot forgive the Nazis. If you could lick my heart, you would be poisoned.'[7] Now we can understand that. What the Nazis did was horrendous. Yet Corrie Ten Boom came out of the Ravensbrück prisoner-of-war camp, where her beloved sister, Betsy, had died at the hands of the Nazis. She returned to Germany after the war, and she spoke about reconciliation and forgiveness that can only be found in Christ. At one particular meeting she saw a man coming towards her, and recognised that he was one of the soldiers who had been in charge of the prisoner-of-war camp where her sister, Betsy, had died. When he came to her with his arm extended, she said to

---

[7] Elie Wiesel, during a television interview, relating his experience of being in Auschwitz during the Second World War.

herself, 'Lord, I cannot forgive this man. Please help me.' He said to her, 'My sister, Corrie, will you please forgive me?' She put out her hand as well and prayed, 'God help me.' And God, she said, provided the words. 'I forgive you, brother,' she said, 'with my whole heart.'[8]

Thirdly, it is possible for a Christian to say, 'I cannot forgive,' yet to really mean, 'I won't forgive.' If you are forgiven, you will forgive. To harbour resentment and say, 'I won't forgive,' has great peril for your soul. How hard it is to forgive when you have been scarred physically, emotionally or even sexually. Ask God to help you so that you can say, like Stephen, 'Lord, do not hold this sin against them.'[9] Or as Paul says, 'Forgive one another as God in Christ has forgiven you.'[10]

I put it to you, in the light of verses 12, 14 and 15 of Matthew 6, that it is impossible to interpret the words of the Lord Jesus in the following way: that you can claim forgiveness by God and continue bearing grudges against your parents, against family members, against those who hurt you, against people in the church, against people outside the church. It is impossible to claim forgiveness and yet, at the same time, go on with a proud determination to be unforgiving in certain circumstances.

Be careful of this attitude. It is the testimony of some older Christians that they can become unbelievers in little ways as they grow older. The memory lengthens and deposits can be made increasingly to the bank of grudges. Slights that you thought you had forgotten come back to you in your old age. You remember why you don't talk to this or that person. You remember why you have something against them. You remember a broken word. You remember an unpaid debt. In your old age you get resentful and vengeful, and a sign of this is that you become increasingly cynical, and critical of people. This is the Third Act of your life. In Act Three, you can become determined that judgment should

---

[8] Story can be found at http://www.odyssey.on.ca/~paul.buis/frpius/ref28.html
[9] Acts 7:60
[10] Ephesians 4:32, Colossians 3:13

triumph over mercy. And so, when the last decisive Act of life comes and the curtain comes down in the finale, you look to the king, and he gives you over to the jailer – everlastingly.

I can remember walking to primary school every day. I attended Clovelly Public School in Sydney, and to get there I had to pass both the Infants' School, and the Girls' Department. I was just learning to read. There was a sign on Arden Street, outside the Girls' Department, which read, 'Trespassers Forgiven' ... well, that is what I *thought* it said. It actually said 'Trespassers Forbidden.' It wouldn't actually have made much sense the other way, would it? It would be like saying, 'Come on, trespass, you are going to be forgiven anyway!' Now, if you were to have a similar sign hung around your neck, would it say 'Trespasses Forgiven', or would it say 'Trespasses Forbidden'? In the first, mercy triumphs; in the second, justice. This is how my heavenly Father will treat each of you unless you forgive your brother from your heart.

Our heavenly Father, forgive us our debts as we have forgiven our debtors.

CHAPTER FIVE

WHY NOT ACCUMULATE?

MATTHEW 6:19-24

In Matthew, chapter 6, verses 19-24, our Lord Jesus says:

> [19]Do not store up for yourselves treasures on earth, where moth and rust destroy, and where thieves break in and steal. [20]But store up for yourselves treasures in heaven, where moth and rust do not destroy, and where thieves do not break in and steal. [21]For where your treasure is, there your heart will be also.
>
> [22]The eye is the lamp of the body. If your eyes are good, your whole body will be full of light. [23]But if your eyes are bad, your whole body will be full of darkness. If then the light within you is darkness, how great is that darkness!
>
> [24]No one can serve two masters. Either he will hate the one and love the other, or he will be devoted to the one and despise the other. You cannot serve both God and money.

Some time ago, there was devastating news here in Australia. The December quarter figures for the gross domestic product had actually gone through negative growth. But we also heard some good news, if you were a Telstra shareholder. Telstra pleased the markets and the price of shares went up. Goodman

Fielder, however, and St George Bank, did not please the markets and their price went down. The little battler, the Aussie dollar, struggled to just above 50 US cents. I thought, in the light of all that economic news, is that all we are as a nation? Is there anything more significant that can be said about Australia apart from the resilience, health, or otherwise of our economy? Is there anything more that can be said of you or me apart from that which can be said of us as producers and consumers? Is there more to life than economics, since economics is the key to political power these days?

The reality is that money is a very useful servant, but it is a very dangerous and destructive master. For those in ministry, or those contemplating ministry, do not think you will be exempt from this.

The most popular song that was sung at the Katoomba Christian Men's Convention a few years ago was that great hymn by William Williams, *Guide Me O Thou Great Jehovah*. The last verse, sung with great vigour at the Convention, goes like this:

> When I tread the verge of Jordan
> Bid my anxious fears subside
> Death of death and hell's destruction
> Land me safe on Canaan's side.

I wonder, if we were going to sing that according to our real hopes and aspirations, whether or not we would sing something like this:

> Death of death and hell's destruction
> Land *my safe* on Canaan's side!

Wouldn't it be wonderful to be able to take it all with you and to have it on the other side?

Well, in this tug of war, in the accumulation of the treasures of earth and the treasures of heaven, it is probable that we are all trying to do both. When you contemplate your budget and ask, 'How much should I save? How much should I give away?', the question really is, 'Where is your heart?' Because that is where your treasure is also. You cannot be in two places at once. And your heart cannot be in two places at once. You might be like the monkey that puts its hand into the jar to get the peanut, but it cannot get its hand out of the jar while it holds the peanut. It wants its freedom from the jar and it wants the peanut as well. We want the riches of earth and the riches of heaven as well.

In this section from Matthew, chapter 6, the Lord Jesus uses three pictures; verse 19, the picture of treasure; verse 22, the picture of the eye, or perspective; and verse 24, the picture of the slave and two masters. But notice the wider context here in chapter 6. It's not just about money. It's about esteem. It's about winning the approval of people. For example, Jesus says in chapter 6, verse 1, 'Don't give in order to engender public approval.' In verse 5 He says, 'Don't pray so that people will think that you are especially godly.' In verse 16 he says, 'When you are fasting, don't do it for public acclaim.' And in verse 19 he says, 'Don't collect wealth so that it will bring you a reputation.' As one early Christian said, 'Nothing so trains men to be fond of riches as the fondness for glory.'[1] We hope that people will somehow respect us because we are wealthy. The Lord Jesus has in mind here materialism as a means to acceptance, esteem, and approval. Instead, our core values, according to chapter 6, verses 9 and 10, should be the honour of God's name, His kingdom coming and His will being done. It is really not our esteem, but it is God's esteem, which is to be our key concern.

Jesus gives us four reasons why we should not be earthly accumulators.

The first, in verse 19, is because earthly accumulation does not last. It rots. Moths eat your clothes. Rust destroys your crops. Thieves (literally Jesus talks about them as 'diggers') break in – they come under the wall and they dig up through the dirt

---

[1] John Chrysostom, *Homilies on Matthew*, 'Homily XX'; text available at http://www.ccel.org/fathers2/NPNF1-10/npnf1-10-26.htm#P2111_699477

– and they steal your gold. In Jesus' day assets were generally held in the form of cloth, grain or gold. These days we hold the Aussie dollar, the US dollar, or stocks. But even they do not last. Jesus does not want his disciples to be disappointed. In verse 19, he says, 'Do not store up for yourselves.' Wealth on earth decays, and as it does it makes you anxious.

In 2001, the Murdoch family gathered in New York, where Rupert Murdoch talked about what it is like to turn 70. He made some joking remarks, and then one reporter asked him, 'No, really. Tell us. How do you feel about turning 70?' And he replied with a one-word response. It could have been a headline from any of his newspapers. He said, 'Bad! I've wasted half my life. That's how I feel – bad.' The tragedy of a life misspent. You would want him to read Proverbs 23:

> [4]Do not wear yourself out to get rich;
> have the wisdom to show restraint.
> [5]Cast but a glance at riches, and they are gone,
> for they will surely sprout wings
> and fly off to the sky like an eagle.

What does the Lord Jesus say? 'Don't live to accumulate earthly treasure, because it rots.'

Then Jesus goes on and gives the second reason why we are not to be earthly accumulators. In verse 20, he says that our purpose is to store up treasure in heaven – to send riches on ahead to eternity. In eternity nothing rots, moth and rust do not destroy, there are no diggers who are going to dig down and break in and steal. So the Lord Jesus says, 'You live to do things on earth which constitute deposits for eternity. Get wealth that is useful for eternity.'

We know we cannot earn our salvation, we know that we are spiritually secure because of God's choice of us, but we are to live in the light of eternity. In chapters 5 and 6 this theme comes up repeatedly in the Sermon on the Mount. In chapter 5, verse 12,

Jesus says, 'Rejoice and be glad because great is your reward in heaven.' There is a reward coming in heaven. In chapter 5, verse 46, he says, 'If you love those who love you, what reward will you get?' In chapter 6, verse 4, he says about giving, 'Then your heavenly Father sees what is done in secret and will reward you.' And in chapter 6, verse 6, with regard to prayer, Jesus says, 'But when you pray, go into your room, close the door, and pray to your Father who is unseen. Then your Father, who sees what is done in secret, will reward you.' There is a reward coming, and we are to be living on earth now with a view to that reward. So, as Martin Luther said, we are to earn money in order to meet the needs of others. We are to be living for God's approval, not people's approval.

We do not know how the rich man in Luke, chapter 16, became rich. Was it that he made good investments in land or crops? But the Lord Jesus says that when he died, he became dreadfully poor because he neglected the only real investment he could have made for eternity. What is the eternal investment the rich man could have made? It was in the beggar, Lazarus, sitting at his gate. The rich man could not take his crops with him. He could not take his cattle with him. He could not take his real estate with him. So what does go into eternity? People go into eternity; but the rich man had made no investment in people for eternity. Lazarus went to the bosom of Abraham. The rich man, however, had made no investment in Lazarus. So the rich man went to hell. Later in Matthew's Gospel Jesus says, 'I was hungry, I was thirsty, I had no clothes, I was in prison, and you fed me, you gave me drink, you clothed me and you visited me.'[2] This is eternal wealth, and this sort of investment in people will suffer no loss; so work for eternal riches.

The third reason Jesus gives is in verse 21, where he says, 'Where your treasure is, there your heart will be also.' The treasure is the magnet for the heart. If you esteem recognition, then ambition

---

[2] Matthew 25:31-46

will take charge of your life. If you esteem money, then greed will take charge of your life. If you esteem pleasure, indulgence will take charge of your life. But if you esteem heaven, service of others in Christ's name will take charge of your heart.

I remember that when our children were young, my father gave me a video camera. It was a prized possession. It was to take videos of our children. I can remember opening the video camera and thinking, 'How can we leave this at home when we go out? Because thieves could break in and steal our priceless video camera. So, when we go out, we will have to put the video camera in the boot. But when we get out of the car, how will we know that thieves won't break into the car and take the video camera out of the boot of the car?' That was nearly twenty years ago. The video camera is now collecting dust at the bottom of the wardrobe. It doesn't work. (I never really could make it work!) But, you see, what is it worth now? It is just an old video camera. Before that, when we left our parish in Wee Waa in 1981, they gave us an old movie camera, an old reel-to-reel movie camera to take movies of the children. Now that really is ancient history! But now it's gone, it's rotted. Things don't last. You can allow yourself to be kidnapped by your possessions. We need to be careful of that. I was given a barbecue in 1995. I should have looked after it. But I turned it on a while ago, and the jolly thing had fallen apart. It didn't last: the wire in it had rotted away. Things do not last – but people do. We go on for eternity. So, treasure God; and if you treasure God, you will treasure people.

Do you know what the Booths, the founders of the Salvation Army, took as their lifelong motto? They gave 'Blood and Fire' to the Salvation Army they founded. That was the motto of the Army. But for themselves, their motto was one word: 'Others'.

The first three reasons to send riches on ahead to heaven are: that heavenly accumulation keeps; that earthly accumulation rots; and that the earthly things kidnap your heart. Jesus tells us the fourth reason in verse 24, when he says, 'You cannot serve two masters. You cannot serve both God and wealth.' To serve wealth is to ignore God, because these two masters, God and wealth, give you contrary orders. James says that too: 'Friendship with the world is enmity towards God.'[3] In verse 24 Jesus makes it quite clear: he starts with the word 'no-one' and then he finishes with 'you cannot'. As part of God's creation, we have been made to serve Him. To serve wealth, which rots, is unworthy of us.

Cyprian, the bishop of Carthage who died in AD 257, wrote about the state of the church under persecution by the Roman Emperor Decius. This is what he said:

> Individuals were applying themselves to the increase of wealth; and forgetting both what was the conduct of believers under the apostles, and what ought to be their conduct in every age, they with insatiable eagerness for gain devoted themselves to the multiplying of possessions ... Numerous bishops ... hunted the markets for mercantile profits; tried to amass large sums of money while they had brethren starving within the church.[4]

We need to be careful because we cannot serve two masters.

What then is the place of verses 22 and 23, where Jesus uses the third picture: the eye? The eye was understood to be the organ of perspective. It is through the eye that you get your world-view. It is the eye that governs the way you live. It is the eye that is the lamp of the body. There is a direct connection between the eye's perspective and the body's behaviour. As you see through the eye, and understand, so you will live consistently with that understanding. So, we must be careful about our attitude, aware that the eye leads us. In Psalm 119, verses 36 and 37, the psalmist says this, as his prayer to God:

---

[3] James 4:4

[4] 'The worldliness of Christians', in WHC Frend and J Stevenson (eds), *A New Eusebius: Documents Illustrating the History of the Church to AD 337*, SPCK Publishing, London, 1987, p p. 215-216.

[36]Turn my heart toward your statutes
And not toward selfish gain.
[37]Turn my eyes away from worthless things;
Preserve my life according to your word.

'Turn my eyes away' – away from worthless things, away from things that will rot. Turn them to what will never rot and never depreciate – which, supremely, is God and his Word. I think if there is one song that sums up what the Christian life is about, it is the one that says this:

O soul are you wearied and troubled,
No light in the darkness you see,
There's light for a look at the Saviour
And life more abundant and free.

Then, the chorus; and here are the words that you should always be saying to yourself:

Turn your eyes upon Jesus,
Look full in his wonderful face,
And the things of earth will grow strangely dim
In the light of his glory and grace.[5]

I need to keep turning my eyes upon Jesus. As I look at my possessions, my superannuation, or whatever: 'Turn your eyes upon Jesus'. Don't be greedy: 'Look full in his wonderful face'. Don't let earthly treasure capture your heart: 'And the things of earth will grow strangely dim in the light of his glory and grace'. Get your eyes right, get your perspective right, and that will control the way you live. But, the question is, what are we to fill our eyes with? Matthew, chapter 6, verse 9, tells you what to fill your eyes with:

Our Father in heaven,
Hallowed be your name,

---

[5] Helen Lemmel, © Copyright 1922, 1950, Singspiration. USA.

¹⁰Your kingdom come,
Your will be done
   On earth as it is in heaven.

That is what we are to fill our eyes with – God's honour, the honour of His name, and the coming of His kingdom. God is no person's debtor. We can trust Him, and depend on Him to watch over our needs. We are to use our wealth to secure His kingdom and His will being done on earth.

Now we come to the application of the passage – the most difficult part. This is where heresy is most often taught. Let me give you what I think is the impossible application of this passage. It is impossible for God's people to live striving to be rich, to have earthly riches occupy our time and our best efforts. If you are a citizen of God's kingdom, that is an impossible lifestyle for you. It is impossible, if you are a citizen of God's kingdom, to simply live to accumulate worldly riches. If you respond by saying, 'Well, I'm only doing it for the family,' you are fooling yourself. You are denying yourself to your family, which is your primary responsibility before God. I would guess that a large number of people today are living according to this impossible application, and are seeking to serve both masters. Wealth is a lawful thing. You may not be guilty of theft. You may not be guilty of adultery. You may not be guilty of hatred. Those are clearly sinful things. But subtle worldliness is a more effective enemy of Christian integrity. You can be greedy. You can be greedy if you are as rich as Rupert Murdoch, or even if you are poor like the poorest member of your church. Beware of being absorbed in the lifelong selfish accumulation of riches.

Origen, a third-century Christian leader, spoke of Christians as money-changers who take the capital of earth and change it into the currency of heaven. How do we do that? The Lord Jesus tells us, in the necessary application of this passage. It is by resisting the gods of the world, and by serving the living and true God – by making eternal investments in people who have an eternal existence, so often ignored by the world. The world knows it is terrible to murder someone, to kill the body – and it is terrible. But we see it with this perspective: that it is terrible to fail to speak the truth, and thus to risk that person's soul continuing to apathetically ignore God, and enter into an eternity of hell. We need to see with an eternal perspective – people are eternal – and we need to make investments in the lives of people, to help them come to live appropriately as citizens of God's kingdom.

Imagine that in my pocket I have thousands of dollars. My investments have paid well recently. But if I go out with this money – Monopoly money, printed by Parker Brothers – it won't even buy me a coffee! It is worthless money, yet at one stage it seemed so important to me. I'd bought Mayfair, I'd got Park Lane, I'd put hotels on each, I'd wiped everybody else out, and still I was rich! Then we closed the Monopoly box, and I went back to living the way I always live, in relative poverty. One day, with what I have from this world, God will close the box on this life. I will stand before Him with some real estate, with some money, with some stocks, with a pension, and God will say, 'Empty out your pockets.' And none of those things falling out of my pockets will have any eternal worth. It will be as useful as Parker Brothers' Monopoly money is here in our economy. I could have my pockets stuffed with Australian dollars, and when I get to heaven God would say, 'That's irrelevant. It won't buy you a cup of coffee here.' Are *you* making eternal investments? Are *you* using wealth to serve others in His name?

Consider how the Lord Jesus goes on to apply this teaching, in verse 25: 'Therefore I tell you,' – if these things are true, which they are – 'don't worry about your life, what you will eat or drink; or about your body, what you will wear.' How you look is not to be your focus. 'Is not life more important than food, and the body more important than clothes? Look how God provides for the birds of the air. Look how he provides for the lilies of the field.' So if those things are not to be the focus of our attention, what is to be the focus of our attention? In verse 32 Jesus says, 'For the pagans run after all these things' – that is, they are concerned about these things – 'and your heavenly Father knows that you need them. But *you* ...' – and here is the big difference that should set us apart – 'you seek his kingdom first, and his righteousness, and all these things will be given to you as well.'

That is what we are to do: to strive for God's kingdom. God's honour, God's will being done and God's kingdom coming first are to be our great concerns. We are not to be driven by the treasure of earthly possessions, earthly acceptance, earthly esteem, or money. If God gives us those things, we are to use them shrewdly to extend His kingdom.

The impossible application of this passage is to mouth our praise of God, but live for the praise of others. In the economy of heaven, it is others who should be our great concern. In the Monopoly economy of this life, you are encouraged to live for yourself, but that is inconsistent with being a citizen of the kingdom.

I once received an email from a couple of our College's graduates who are missionaries in Thailand. I always enjoy getting their emails because they are always particularly challenging. In this one they talked about what is really good about being missionaries. They mentioned various things like the cheapness of food, and the children having a personal tutor, their mother, who trains and educates them. They are good things, they said, but they are not the best thing. They wrote:

> The best thing about being a missionary is the spiritual blessings we receive from doing the work of the gospel. This is measured by the fact that we live in a community that loves and supports one another. It comes out in people's lives as they live to serve, rather than to accumulate a whole lot of stuff. Imagine what benefits we gain from living in such a community, being with a group of people where serving God is more important than getting a good education, where serving people is more important than a career or a bigger house, where our children live in an environment where it is

normal for people to spend their whole energy working for God's kingdom.

That is the norm. As one of our own poets, Michael Card, has said:

> And it's hard to imagine the freedom we find
> From the things we leave behind.[6]

In the front of my Bible I keep various things. There is a family photo that is now a bit out of date, or it will be soon. I've got my favourite hymn. I've got my favourite letter from the *Sydney Morning Herald* letters page. And I have these words:

> When I reach the end of my days a moment or two from now, I must look backward on something more meaningful than the pursuit of houses and land and stocks and bonds. I will consider my earthly existence to have been wasted unless I can recall a loving family, a consistent investment in the lives of people and an earnest attempt to serve the God who made me. Nothing else makes much sense.[7]

'When I reach the end of my days a moment or two from now ...'. Let us live now with a view to that moment.

---

[6] Michael Card, from his song 'Things We Leave Behind'., *Poiema*, The Sparrow Corporation, 1994.

[7] Dr J. Dobson, quoted on Focus on the Family website, http://dvlp.family.org/fofmag/pf/a0029038.cfm

CHAPTER SIX

SELF-DELUSION

MATTHEW 7:24-29

In Matthew, chapter 7, verse 24 to the end of the chapter, Jesus talks about the issue of self-delusion. He says:

> [24]'Therefore everyone who hears these words of mine and puts them into practice is like a wise man who built his house on the rock. [25]The rain came down, the streams rose, and the winds blew and beat against that house; yet it did not fall, because it had its foundation on the rock. [26]But everyone who hears these words of mine and does not put them into practice is like a foolish man who built his house on sand. [27]The rain came down, the streams rose, and the winds blew and beat against that house, and it fell with a great crash'
>
> [28]When Jesus had finished saying these things, the crowds were amazed at his teaching, [29]because he taught as one who had authority, and not as their teachers of the law.

On one occasion in the mid-1980s, my wife Maxine and I were invited to go to a small country town in the north-west of New South Wales, where the Gideons of the northern district of the state were having their annual conference. It was held at the local RSL Club.[1] On the first Saturday morning of the event, they publicised next year's conference, which was to be held at a beachside resort in Coffs Harbour. As we sat there in the RSL Club, I said to Maxine, 'We came one year too early! We should have been here next year'. She agreed. A couple of years later, we were invited to the National Convention of the Gideons. The letter said, 'We will look after your accommodation, your travel costs, etc. The last paragraph said the National Convention was to be held at a Sydney suburban civic centre, just down the road from where we live at Croydon! It was a bit of a disappointment.

However, the phone rang shortly afterwards. It was Los Angeles calling.

'We'd like to invite you to our church.'

'Oh, do you want me to preach?'

'No, we don't want you to preach. At our church in Los Angeles, which is very close to Disneyland, we have three services on a Sunday: one at 9 a.m., one at 10.30 a.m. and one at 7 p.m. We want you to take part in the 10.30 a.m. service. We'll look after your accommodation in a five-star hotel for five nights, and you and your wife will have your air fares paid'

'Well, if you don't want me to preach, what is it you want me to do?'

'At the 10.30 a.m. service, which is televised nationally, we want you to pray.'

'You want me to pray?'

Now, unfortunately, that second invitation did not come to me. It actually came to an English Christian biographer, Norman Grubb. But you would have to think that this must be a significant prayer, for him to be taken from half-way across the world just to pray at a 10.30 a.m. church service on American television. This was the prayer:

---

[1] The Returned and Services League of Australia, an organization serving veterans and those interested in Australia's military heritage.

Good morning, Lord.
What are you up to today?
May I be a part of it?
Amen.

Aren't you sorry you didn't think of that! It's an interesting prayer of Norman Grubb's, isn't it, because it raises a good question. What is God up to today? Is God doing anything new today that He wasn't doing yesterday? God's not up to anything new: as always, God is up to honouring His Son by making a people like Him. And you, if you are a Christian, are a part of that people. But how is God making us like Jesus and therefore honouring His Son? He does it through the circumstances of life. Both the good things and the not-so-good things that happen to us are designed to make us like Jesus. We have the assurance that all these circumstances are designed by God to see us 'conformed to the likeness of his Son'.[2]

However, the great instrument that God uses to make us like his Son is His Word, the Bible. It teaches us, it rebukes us, it corrects us. Martin Luther said, 'The Bible is alive; it speaks to me; it has feet, it runs after me; it has hands, it lays hold of me'.[3] God's great purpose for us is our growing to be like Him; so it is crucial for us to spend significant time in His Word, the Bible. Whether we are spending time in the Bible personally, or in a class lecture at Bible college, or as a church, it is important and significant.

But the great danger when we spend time in God's Word is the danger of self-delusion. James says to his readers, 'Do not merely listen to the word, and delude yourselves, rather, do what the word says'.[4]

In Matthew, chapter 7, the context of these words of Jesus is His teaching about choices. In verse 13 there are two ways;

---

[2] Romans 8:29
[3] Quote available at http://www.piety hilldesign.com/gcq/quotespages/bible.html
[4] See James 1:22-25.

there is the narrow way and the broad way. 'Enter through the narrow gate,' He says, 'for wide is the gate and broad is the road that leads to destruction'. He then goes on to contrast these two ways with two kinds of prophets, in verse 15: 'Watch out for the false prophets'. The false prophets and the true prophets then correspond to two types of trees. In verse 17 He says, '... every good tree bears good fruit, but a bad tree bears bad fruit'. So He puts before us two ways, two types of prophets, and two types of trees. Then, in verse 21, Jesus says there are two types of people professing faith: 'Not everyone who says to me, "Lord, Lord," will enter the kingdom of heaven, but only he who does the will of my Father who is in heaven.'

It is in the context of these contrasts – two ways, two prophets, two trees, two professions of faith – that Jesus begins, in verse 24, to talk about two builders, the wise builder and the foolish builder. However, what is significant for us is the setting in which Jesus tells the story. It is at the end of His Sermon on the Mount, and you can imagine people saying, 'Thanks, Lord, that was a great message. We were encouraged when we heard you say we are to love our enemies, we are to turn the other cheek, and we are not to look lustfully on a person of the opposite sex. We were encouraged when you urged us to pray, "Forgive us as we forgive others." We were greatly encouraged when you told us that we are to accumulate for heaven and not for earth'.

But Jesus replies, 'Stop! Before you go any further, let me tell you a story'. And here is the story, for people just like us: people who have heard the Lord Jesus through this magnificent Sermon on the Mount. There was a wise builder, who was going to build a house. Where did he build his house? Well, like anyone, 'position, position, position'! That is what he was after. He got the right architectural design, the right colour scheme and the right foundation. Good foundations are very important, and this man found a rock to build his house upon.

I remember when we were building the extension to Wallace House, currently our women's quarters at College, and we had $100,000 to start the building. Every day I would go up see the builder, to monitor the progress he was making. I can vividly remember the day when the falling account balance indicated we had already spent $50,000. I spoke to the builder, and he said, 'You look disappointed.'

I said, 'Today, we've spent $50,000, and I can't see anything.'

'What did you expect to see?'

'I expected some bricks above the ground: something, anything, even a window.'

He said, 'Listen, mate. These foundations are very solid, and this building will be here long after you and I are gone.'

The foolish builder is a clear contrast to the wise builder. The fool also looks for position, architectural design and colour schemes; but what is it that the fool disregards? He disregards the foundation. I mean, why worry about what you cannot see? If you pick up the property section of Saturday's *Sydney Morning Herald* and look at all the advertisements for real estate, what do you see? 'Renovator's delight' (that is an automatic warning, isn't it); 'close to amenities'; 'close to public transport'. What you don't see in those advertisements is any reference to the house's foundation. Why? Because we take the foundation for granted. When a house is being inspected, I look around and I think, 'This a nice house'. But I never think to say, 'Hey, pull up the floorboards and let me have a look underneath'. You just assume that it is OK down there. So why pour money into what cannot be seen? Surely you are better off introducing a new colour scheme than putting in better foundations. You will get better resale value!

Now the fool, you see, thinks that he is wise. But notice what Jesus says in verse 27: He says that the rain came down against each of those homes. Simply because you are wise it does not mean that the storms of life will not come against you. The house of the fool collapsed, 'and it fell with a great crash'; but the house of the wise builder stood firm. In verse 25 Jesus says, 'The rain came down, the streams rose, and the winds blew and beat against that house; yet it did not fall'. Why? Because it had its firm foundation on the rock. Jesus goes on to make the point Himself. He gives us the contrast between verse 26 and verse 24, between 'everyone who hears these words of mine and *does not* put them into practice', and 'everyone who hears these words of mine and *does* put them into practice'. The wise person is wise because he or she recognises the reality that God's Word is to be heard and done. The foolish person is a fool because he or she thinks God's Word is only to be heard. Notice that these two types of people are identical at the point of input. They both get their Christian books from the same bookshops, they both listen to the same CD messages from Katoomba Christian Convention. Yet one is a fool while the other is wise. One is truly wise, but the other is self-deluded. The wise recognise that God's Word is to be heard *and* put into practice.

We have to be careful about that, haven't we, because here in Sydney we hear good biblical teaching so much of the time. It seems to me that in Sydney we emphasise that if you want to grow and be godly you have to have good teaching. But often the way we talk about this good teaching is the way we talk about having a shower to be clean. If I want to be clean, I get into the shower, I wash myself, lather myself up, wash it all off, and I'm clean. The more I shower, the cleaner I am. So the more often I sit under the ministry of the teaching of God's Word, the more godly I'll become. But it doesn't happen like that. Therefore this is a particularly appropriate message for those of us who enjoy the privilege of receiving faithful Bible teaching: we must also put it into action.

The environment in which Jesus spoke here in the first-century was dominated by one philosophy, called Gnosticism, or 'knowledgism'. Gnosticism held that knowledge was an end in itself: as long as you knew certain secret truths, you would be right with God and you would be right for the hereafter. But Jesus confronts that and says that knowledge is never to be an end in itself. If you merely listen, you will be self-deluded. Yet how apt we are to be self-deluded.

A few years ago, at the College's Biennial Preaching Conference, our guest preacher was Haddon Robinson. On the Saturday afternoon Haddon preached at a reunion for all our graduates. He preached magnificently about King David. He explained how David was good in many ways, but failed abysmally as a family man, as a father to his children. I can remember being deeply convicted about my own fathering. The next morning, our family went to church together, and the pastor said he had just read a journal article that week on 23 ways of being a better father. My kids were sitting behind me and I could feel their eyeballs boring into the back of my head. The pastor said, 'I'm not going to mention all 23 ways of being a better father,' but he started, and it felt to me like he was doing all 23! I sat there feeling guiltier and guiltier about my lack of patience and my lack of involvement. So, I had heard two messages in the one week on being a better father. After church, Maxine and I and our son then went to have lunch with my parents. We left the other children at home with their friends. When we arrived home at about 6 p.m., they went off with Maxine to youth group and church, leaving all the washing-up from lunch still undone. Nobody had lifted a finger to wash up anything. They had had a great afternoon with their friends, and I was left with an eight-year-old boy to do the washing-up. I thought, 'I'm going to discipline those kids when they get home! I'm going to give them a good talking-to as soon as they get into the house!' Then I thought, 'Wait a minute. Maybe there is a connection between this and the two sermons I've heard this morning and yesterday.' But it had taken me about an hour to make that connection. So when the children came home I was in bed, and I didn't lose my patience with them. (But Maxine gave them the talking-to they needed!)

If you are slow like I am, often we don't make connections that are obvious. I was challenged to be a better father; then there was an opportunity to be a good father, and I was very slow to make the connection. And often we don't make connections between what we hear from God's Word and our regular everyday living. Jesus says, 'You will be a self-deluded fool if you merely listen to this sermon and don't do it. But you'll be wise if you listen *and* do it.' That is why the Sermon on the Mount concludes with this warning. Jesus is saying, '*Do* the Sermon on the Mount. This is your spiritual DNA, so live it out'.

You may be thinking, 'Come on, that is a big demand! *Do* the Sermon on the Mount? How can I get a handle on the Sermon on the Mount?' In chapter 6 we find the centre of the Sermon – what it is all about. If I said to you, 'What do you believe?', many of you could rattle off the Apostles' Creed. But if I really wanted to know what you believed in your heart of hearts, if I could get alongside you when you were quite alone and you were praying to God, your praying would tell me what you really believe. By the way you pray, you would be telling me your aspirations, your hopes and your fears. 'Our prayers,' someone has said, 'are our creeds.' If the Sermon on the Mount is about the culture of God's kingdom, then that culture will be most clearly reflected in the way Jesus teaches us to pray. Here are the culture's characteristics in Matthew, chapter 6, beginning at verse 9:

> Our Father in heaven,
> Hallowed be your name,
> [10]Your kingdom come,
> Your will be done on earth as it is in heaven.
> [12]Forgive us our debts,
>   As we also have forgiven our debtors,
> [13]And lead us not into temptation,
> But deliver us from the evil one.

At every point, the Lord's Prayer confronts our Australian culture. First of all, Jesus puts first and foremost our concern for the honouring of God's name. God is to be honoured. Parents of friends of ours went overseas as missionaries later in life. The father was a surgeon. He gathered his children around him before they left and said, 'We've got three things to say to you because we may not come back. One, we want you to love God. Two, keep in contact with one another. And, three, don't argue over the will'. It was good advice. My friend said, 'We knew exactly how to honour our father's remembrance. Love God, love one another, and don't argue about the estate'. Here, in the Lord's Prayer, Jesus is telling us in the clearest terms, 'Make the honouring of God your supreme concern, your key concern'. In Australian culture, when it comes to the honouring of God's name, we are apathetic. Many Australians could not care less. In fact, we will frequently take God's name and abuse it. Our culture is confronted by the culture of God's kingdom, reflected here in this pattern of prayer.

Secondly, he says, 'Your kingdom come, your will be done on earth as it is done in heaven'. In other words, we have a great and certain hope for the future, when God will deliver us from this painful, suffering world. We are people who are waiting, not pessimistically, but optimistically, for the Day. In Australia, at every level of our society, we have deep despair and pessimism. Despair and pessimism mark our nation's life. But as Christians in God's kingdom, we are praying for the Day, the coming of God's kingdom, to break in to earth. We are to be hopeful, expectant, anticipatory people.

Thirdly, we are dependent people; we are not self-made people. We are dependent on God for our physical needs, our daily bread, and also for our spiritual needs. We need forgiveness. 'Forgive us our debts as we have forgiven our debtors'. In filling this need, we are not independent. In Australia we think of ourselves as being very independent. It is the mark of the great Australian – the quiet, laconic, independent man. Not so! Just as we are dependent on our heavenly Father for every breath we take, we also depend on Him for the forgiveness of every sin.

Fourthly, we need deliverance, not to be led into temptation but to be delivered from the evil one. Temptation can be so attractive, so desirable – the quick dollar, the easy pornographic magazine, the prospect of the syringe in the arm, the underhanded scheme, illicit sex, the slanderous use of the tongue. It can seem so attractive, so smooth. Our society says, 'Be carefree! You are being stupid, there's nothing more to come! Get it all now!' And Jesus says we need deliverance from that whole worldly system which encourages us to 'just do it'.

In this closing part of the Sermon on the Mount Jesus tells his disciples that we are to see that this culture, as determined by the Lord's Prayer, is obvious among us. Don't just hear these words of Jesus. Don't be led by your Australian culture of apathy and pessimism and independence and carelessness. Instead be penitent and carefully dependent on God, for He says, 'This is the one I esteem, the one who is humble and contrite and who trembles at my word.'[5] Do not be foolish builders; rather, be wise.

You might like to flip back through the previous chapters in this book and review them, because we are often quite resistant to God's Spirit as He leads us in the way of conviction and change. We are, we saw in the first chapter, to be surprising people. We are particularly to be known as those who love others who don't like us. How are you praying for your persecutor, that person who doesn't like you? Are you actually loving that person who doesn't like you? And what about personal retribution? Has there been a decrease in road rage from your point of view? Have you all of a sudden become a more generous user of the road? What about persevering in control of your body? It is so easy to not persevere in the control of our body and our lust. We think that with the passage of time, truth loses its relevance to

---

[5] Isaiah 66:2

us, and so it loses its edge. Are you diligent in forgiving others, or more diligent in making deposits to the bank of grudges? Are you making heavenly investments in people? Or are you still stashing away selfishly for yourself? How have the first six chapters affected the way you pray for your enemies and your persecutors, the way you invest in gospel ministry and in the lives of people, and the way you spend your time?

Sports clubs in Australia were rejoicing after the September 2000 Sydney Olympic Games, because they were doubling their membership in archery and volleyball, and in many other sports too. But later when the colder weather came, a lot of the people who were training to get into the next Olympics were not quite so keen. It's the reality, isn't it? Did you hear what it was like in Sydney during the Games? I wouldn't have been anywhere else on earth. It was amazing! People genuinely seemed to care about each other. Everybody from public transport employees to volunteers were saying 'Good morning!' to everyone. It was just terrific to be together. There we all were, all Australians chanting, 'Aussie, Aussie, Aussie, Oi, Oi, Oi!' It was a thoroughly communal time.

Yet I can remember the morning after the Olympics, driving up the Pacific Highway and listening to the programme 'AM' on ABC Radio. Here we were, a renewed, nationalistic, united nation. And what was the programme about? The fact that the New South Wales Minister for the Olympics thought the head of the Sydney Organising Committee for the Olympic Games should be awarded only a silver medallion, instead of a gold one. Then I listened to our national leaders in Federal Parliament – this is the new nation with a new sense of unity because of the Olympics – and I heard such an uproar and such bickering and politicking there that I was sure it would be in the headlines the next morning. It was appalling behaviour! But it wasn't even mentioned the next day in the newspaper, because it was so typical: it happens every day. Our nation's leaders provided no pattern for our relating in the way they relate to one another, because change cannot come about through a sporting event. Change, real change, only comes by God's Holy Spirit. We need to be prayerful people so that the whole ethos of the Lord's Prayer will dominate our living much more, and so that it will be increasingly obvious that we are kingdom citizens.

If you are a parent, how long has it been since you sat down with your son and prayed for his purity? Or with your daughter, and talked to her about the kingdom of God and the fact that she needs to marry within the kingdom? And particularly fathers: how long has it been since you came home from work early and made significant investments of time in your family? Husbands, how long has it been since you prayed with your wife and showed that your first priority is to present her to God pure and blameless on the Day? And you children, how do you show honour to your parents? Very often, students will come and ask me for some advice on something and I say, 'Have you talked to your parents about this?' We become so independent of our parents. If you have living parents, how do you honour them? Do you still talk to them about issues? Or do you ignore them? They are there to be honoured by you, no matter what age you are. Honour your parents.

Anything in our daily living that makes the kingdom and its culture more obvious is the appropriate application of this passage. All our relationships are to reflect a kingdom passion, our dependence on God, our passion for His honour, our humility, and our need for deliverance, being especially careful about purity. We need to pray that God will bring about real change in us, so that we won't be like the foolish builder, simply self-deluded.

There are two ways, two prophets, two trees, two professions of faith and two builders. Which one are you going to be? You see, Christianity is not just about information: it is about *transformation*. It is not just about challenge: it is about *change*.

It is not just about hearing, it is also about *adhering*. The one who hears the Word and puts it into practice is wise. The one who hears the Word carefully but does not, in prayerful dependence on God, put it into practice, is self-deceived.

Heed these words of Christ!

CHAPTER SEVEN

DID I CHOOSE, OR WAS I CHOSEN?

MATTHEW 11:20-30

The Christian faith is full of apparent contradictions. The first is the last, and the last is first. The way up is down. The way of strength is human weakness. The captive of Christ is the truly free person. The way of conquering and triumph is without the use of human weaponry.

In Matthew 11, verses 20-30, Jesus addresses the paradox of human responsibility and God's sovereignty in salvation. What he says surprises us because he affirms three truths that seem to contradict each other.

The first truth
People are responsible for hardened unrepentance in the face of God's clear revelation of Jesus as the Christ.

> [20]Then Jesus began to denounce the cities in which most of his miracles had been performed, because they did not repent. Woe to you, Korazin! [21]Woe to you Bethsaida! If the miracles that were performed in you had been performed in Tyre and Sidon, they would have repented long ago in sackcloth and ashes.[22]But I tell you, it will be more bearable

for Tyre and Sidon on the day of judgment than for you. ²³And you, Capernaum, will you be lifted up to the skies? No, you will go down to the depths. If the miracles that were performed in you had been performed in Sodom, it would have remained to this day. ²⁴But I tell you that it will be more bearable for Sodom on the day of judgment than for you.

The second truth

God has both a hiding and revealing ministry. We can only know God the Father if his Son reveals Him to us.

> ²⁵At that time Jesus said, I praise you Father, Lord of heaven and earth, because you have hidden these things from the wise and learned and revealed them to little children. ²⁶Yes, Father, for this was your good pleasure.
> ²⁷All things have been committed to me by my Father. No-one knows the Son except the Father, and no-one knows the Father except the Son and those to whom the Son chooses to reveal him.

The third truth

The appeal of Jesus is genuine and universal: that all who hear Him should come to Him and find rest.

> ²⁸Come to me all you who are weary and burdened and I will give you rest. ²⁹Take my yoke upon you and learn from me, for I am gentle and humble in heart and you will find rest for your souls. ³⁰For my yoke is easy and my burden is light.

Why can these verses perplex us? Because we find it difficult to reconcile God's sovereignty in salvation, with His appeal for us to come to Christ. But as Jesus speaks, we see a seamless transition from the responsibility of the cities for their non-repentance (vv. 20-24) to the statement regarding God's sovereignty in human salvation (vv. 25-27), and then to the widespread appeal to come to Christ for rest (vv. 28-30).

People, then, are responsible for their rejection of Christ. He pleads that all would come to Him. There shouldn't be any problem with this – except that it seems to ignore Jesus' second truth, that only God the Father can reveal and save through the Son.

Jesus is the unheeded Christ at this point, because our hearing is selective. Most of us will have experienced a child's selective hearing: children hear what they want to hear. Once, one of our children asked permission to go on an outing. I replied with a conditional yes: 'Yes, you may go provided ...,' but all the child heard was: 'Yes, you may go.' As adults we can have the same tendency. In church, we may hear a preacher say what we want him to say, and once he has said that we switch off and hear no more. So it is here with these three truths from Jesus: we hear the first, we don't really hear the second because it seems contradictory, then we tune in again to the third.

Jesus shocks his Jewish listeners in verses 20-24 by comparing the cities of Israel – Korazin, Bethsaida and Capernaum – to three Gentile cities: Tyre, Sidon and Sodom. If these Gentile cities (which exemplify greed and accumulation, perversion and pride) had had the miracles of Jesus performed in them, they would have repented long before now.

Jesus compares Capernaum to Babylon by quoting Isaiah's description of Babylon ('going down to the depths of the pit,' 14:14-15), then applying it to Capernaum in verse 23. You cities of Israel, he says, so secure in your covenant relationship with God, will be judged severely and even more intolerably than the pagan cities on judgment day, because of your rejection of Jesus the Christ.

The principle here is that the greater the privilege, the greater the responsibility. Israel had great privileges; she had the very words of God (Rom. 3:2), and she had the Messiah walk her streets, performing mighty works. The towns of Korazin and Bethsaida were less than four kilometres apart. There, Jesus fed the 5,000 (Luke 9:10-17). There, the blind man was healed (Mark 8:22-26). It was in Capernaum that Jesus had begun preaching (Matt. 4:13). There, he had healed the centurion's servant, and Simon Peter's mother-in-law and the oppressed and sick (Matt. 8:5-17). Yet in the face of this accreditation of Jesus and clear revelation, there is non-repentance.

So Jesus says that people are responsible for the choices they make, and must bear the consequences.

One of the many stories which emerged after the death of Kerry Packer, Australia's richest man, concerned his late night visit to an English village where he wanted to buy his team a drink and dinner. They turned up at a pub only to be turned away by the publican,[1] as the kitchen had closed. At the next hotel, the owner had similar news but offered to make up some ham sandwiches for the group.

After a pleasant evening the publican presented his bill of £128. Kerry Packer wrote out a cheque for £100,128, the extra £100,000 being the tip. 'Before you bank it', said Packer, 'take it to the other pub at the end of the village and show it to the bloke who wouldn't give us any grub'. It will make a difference to your choices in life when you know who you are dealing with.

Here Jesus speaks of people who don't realise they are rejecting God's Son. These are cities full of people who choose not to respond when Jesus comes to their town; and as a result they will spend eternity under the judgment of God Himself. Jesus has authority from God to reveal the Father; yet He allows people to make choices about Him, and holds them accountable for the choices they make.

Verse 25 now introduces a seemingly contradictory statement, and its first words 'At that time' ... indicate that it is in this context of human accountability that we are confronted with God's sovereignty. But we don't often hear His words in verses 25-28. Why? Because we don't think it is fair that we should be held

---

[1] The owner or manager of a pub.

responsible if only God can determine who should come to know Him. Why then should people be judged if it is God who decides?

Jesus' prayer of thanksgiving in these verses reveals His belief that his Father is Lord of heaven and earth, and that it is His gracious purpose to hide and to reveal.

From whom does He hide things, and to whom does He reveal them? In verse 25, He hides them from the 'wise' and 'learned' – the religious, who think they know everything and have nothing to learn. And he reveals to little children, to people who are childlike, that the kingdom of heaven belongs to such as these (Matt. 19:13-15). These are the meek, merciful, penitent, pure, peacemakers described in the Sermon on the Mount. Supremely they are 'the poor in spirit', the category which heads the list in Matthew 5:3. They have nothing to commend themselves to God – 'nothing in my hand I bring'. Yet to these little children, in all their humble dependence, the Father reveals these things. He is the God who esteems the humble and contrite (Isa. 66:2), the God who is repelled by human self-sufficiency (Isa. 2:11), and the God who is pleased to graciously reveal Himself to the little children. This gives God pleasure, and Jesus shares his Father's pleasure and thanks Him.

In verse 27 Jesus elaborates: there is the most intimate connection between the Father and the Son, so that only the Father really knows the Son, and only the Son really knows the Father.

It can be very frustrating being on the outside of such an intimate relationship. If you have not enjoyed a close relationship with your parents, then observing such closeness that others enjoy can produce feelings of hollowness, frustration, or even envy and anger. But this relationship of God the Father and God the Son is not like that. As intimate as it is, there is an entrance to it for all of us who are on the outside. The frustrated, hollow, envious, outsiders may come in, not on their own terms, but on the terms laid down by the Father and the Son.

To know this intimacy is based on the Lord's choice, 'and anyone to whom the Son chooses to reveal him'. So that for those who come as little children, with zero, nought to offer, a sense of complete poverty of spirit, who do not contribute even the faith, the decision, to come; to these God the Father and God the Son will reveal the truth and bring them into his family.

What then is Jesus saying about our responsibility? We are held responsible for the choices we make. We are powerless to make choices and in fact Jesus chooses us. Sometimes the truest thing to say is to say two true things.

The believer is a person in a relationship of real privilege. We are members of a close family, members who have a relationship with God: 'This is eternal life, that they may know you, the only true God, and Jesus Christ, whom you have sent' (John 17:3). And we don't deserve it, we haven't earned it in any way. We haven't been clever or good enough, but we have received knowledge of a mystery – not by research or philosophical speculation but by revelation. Revelation that is totally undeserved. We could never have worked it out for ourselves: we were in the dark and loved the dark. But now we have a most precious knowledge for which the Lord Jesus thanks God the Father, and for which we ought to be eternally thankful. It is all of God and He does not want you to hold back any of the glory for yourself.

He will not share the spotlight with you, as though He saved you and you had a contribution to make. Even the very repentance and faith you needed to link you to Him is His gift to you. (Acts 11:18; 13:48; 16:14; Eph. 2:8-9; Heb. 12:2). Yet we continue to ignore this central teaching of Jesus, and in our human pride glorify God *and* ourselves for our salvation.

The charge that is commonly made against Jesus' words in verses 25-27 is that these verses paralyse the believer at the point of evangelistic witness. It is sometimes alleged that if we believe that salvation is ultimately a result of God's choice, not ours, then we will sit back and leave the work of reaching the lost to God.

Nothing could be further from the truth. In fact, we persevere in evangelism because our trust is in God, the great evangelist, to do his work through human witness. If our trust were in people's ability to see the truth then we could well be discouraged. Rather we believe that our task is fruitful because of God's choice, so we persist in sharing the gospel.

In Matthew 11:28-30, Jesus couples the necessity of God's choice, with the wide invitation for His listeners to choose. There is nothing limited, narrow or miserly about verses 28-29. 'Come to me all you who are weary and burdened, and I will give you rest. Take my yoke upon you and learn from me, for I am gentle and humble in heart and you will find rest for your souls.'

Jesus' third truth renews the appeal that would have been heard by those in the cities of Korazin, Bethsaida and Capernaum. He calls on all the weary and burdened (that is, all of us) to come to Him and find rest. But then, in verse 29, we notice that He refers to a yoke, normally a heavy, oppressive burden. Surely the burdened are already heavily burdened enough. Surely they do not need another yoke to add to their load. Surprisingly though, Jesus describes his yoke as easy.

Jesus is talking about those who are labouring under the heavy load of obedience to the law (see Acts 15:10). But in coming to Him, they don't come to a set of regulations, but to a person; they come to learn from Him, a gentle and humble master. To be in relationship with such a one is indeed an easy yoke and a light burden. Jesus offers rest (or refreshment or relief) from guilt, from frustration, and the anxiety of never meeting impossible demands.

Twice Jesus promises such relief: in verse 28, 'I will give you rest', and in verse 29, 'you will find rest for your souls'. In knowing Him there is rest. These are indeed 'comfortable words' as the Anglican Book of Common Prayer states. So He returns to the yoke in verse 30, and says it is easy and light.

Among the treasured mementos in my Bible is a copy of one of my favourite hymns, written by Horatius Bonar:

I heard the voice of Jesus say come unto me and rest;
Lay down thou weary one, lay down thy head upon my breast.

I came to Jesus as I was, weary and worn and sad;
I found in him my resting place and he has made me glad.

We have acknowledged that our problem is that we tend to hear Jesus selectively. Either we hear verses 20-24 and 28-30, and stress the importance of *human choice*. (That then becomes all-important, for to make the wrong choice in relation to Jesus is to make an eternal mistake.) Or alternatively, we hear only verses 25-27, and stress the supremacy of *God's choice*: that unless God chooses there is no possibility of revelation and relationship with God. Jesus is the unheeded Christ when we listen to Him selectively, and do not hear both truths at the same time.

When we hear Jesus speak these two truths at the same time, what will it look like? In my last parish in Sydney, the church decided to visit one street in the area on the third Sunday afternoon of each month. The same street, once a month, for a year. Each month we carried a different gospel tract and tried to organise ourselves so that the same couple visited the same home each time. For a traditional parish church this was certainly a different approach. We all gathered to pray, then some stayed to pray that Jesus would reveal the Father, while others went out with the gospel to urge residents to repent and turn to Christ. We applied both truths which Jesus said, at once.

Jesus is unheeded when we don't hear Him say that human choices are real. An overemphasis on God's sovereignty results in apathy, ill-discipline and irresponsibility.

A newsletter from the leader of a school's Christian Fellowship, seeking to portray the normality of Christians, writes, 'We are like everyone else, we smoke and drink too much and disobey our parents'. Are we just like everyone else? This was a group that was well-taught about God's election and sovereign choice. This newsletter betrayed the attitude, 'We are the elect, God has chosen us, so we'll be right.' God's sovereign choice is so emphasised that personal discipline and saying 'no' to ungodliness and 'yes' to godliness become irrelevancies, and hypocrisy is bred. The warnings of Jesus of verses 20-24 go unheeded.

Kirk Patston, Senior Old Testament Lecturer at Sydney Missionary and Bible College, has written:

My wife often comments to me that she feels like she has reached a place in her Christian life when few people hold her accountable anymore. And I think I know what she means. People can start to see you as a professional Christian. You have been to the right colleges, you go to the right church, you are seen at the right conferences. You are even clever enough with your exegetical skills to explain away Bible passages that used to make you feel uncomfortable. And so the challenge to keep choosing repentance and faith can disappear from your life.

Most people these days will move to a new town or city at some stage in their life. And at those times of disruption, it will be easy for you to say, 'Oh, I've been surrounded by the Bible for years. Yes, I'm going to get involved in a local church, but I just need some space. I'm not actually going to get involved in a Bible study group for a few years.' You might subscribe to Scripture Union notes to help you keep your Bible reading habits, but they will arrive and you will think; 'Oh, I have heard all this before, this is just boring repetition.' And you will start to grow indifferent about applying the Scriptures to your own life. You will start to think that your decisions don't really matter that much, that God will hang on to you because you are one of his people. And Jesus will tell you to control your tongue, and you will say, 'Oh maybe another time. It's not as though my status with you, Jesus, is under threat.' And Jesus will say, 'You are slowly giving into a love of money.' And you will say, 'Jesus, just give me some space.' You might arrive at the point in your Christian life where you have lost any sense that choices matter, that choices shape the future, that choices have consequences. Jesus' strong words here about the real choice that people can make to be wrong about him, come as an important warning to us.

But remember also the opposite danger of not hearing Jesus when He says that He *chooses* people (vv. 25-27). This is evident clearly in our secularism. We simply live and minister without regard for God. We don't pray. Prayer is the clearest sign that we take Jesus' words of verses 25-27 seriously. If our confidence is purely in our own ability to persuade, or our listener's ability to be persuaded, if we are the highest authorities, then we should pray to our listeners and prepare our arguments well! But the reality is, without God, our work is in vain. By praying we acknowledge our dependence on God and His sovereignty. The environment in which we live and minister needs to be an environment of prayer, for the effectiveness of our work depends on the Lord Jesus 'choosing to reveal him'. Pray that He will.

If we don't hear the truth of verses 25-27, our ministry becomes simply the marketing of a product. To make the gospel more consumer–friendly we will be urged to adopt the latest business, management and marketing agendas, cutting any talk of God's wrath, hell or the need to repent. Conversion may be seen as a merely human choice, the equivalent to signing a contract, and discipleship seen as a human enterprise.

Further, neglecting verses 25-27 will lead us to become discouraged by the hardness of people. We will write off whole groups of people who seem too resistant to the gospel. Areas of our cities will become no-go zones for the gospel, because the 'types' who live there aren't the types to become Christian. Whole industries will be neglected – the politician, the professional sportsperson, those involved in the entertainment industry. The wealthy professionals will be neglected, as well as the 'down and outers'. We will become progressively middle-classed, and the Bible belt will become denser and narrower.

But remember God is the great evangelist. His heart is for the lost and He has no pleasure in the death of the wicked.

Jesus' sovereign choice is made as we take His invitation into a despairing world:

> 'Come to me all you who are weary and burdened and I will give you rest.' And Jesus will reveal the Father; you, reader, are the proof of that!

I find that the Father is more willing to reveal than I am to speak, for when I speak I seldom find people who are not willing to talk in some way. God has prepared the way and opened up the conversation.

So what will it mean for you to listen to both these truths at the same time? It will mean that you will commit the day to God in expectant prayer that He may open up all sorts of intersections and conversations for you: in the bus, the train, the surgery or the hairdresser's chair. That as you speak, God may prepare the way for revealing Himself. You will recognise that these encounters are not coincidences, but divinely organised intersections.

You may arm yourself with an engaging gospel tract to leave with people. You will pray, and you will be ready to seize the moment for opportunistic witness.

Take that friend or associate in the office, who over the years has seemed so hardened to the gospel: you won't give up on them but will persist in seeking to show them love and goodwill, and to share the gospel with them.

The night before His death, Jesus told His disciples that they were to testify to the world. This is what He said:

> When the Counsellor comes whom I will send to you from the Father, the Spirit of Truth who goes out from the Father, he will testify about me. And you also must testify, for you have been with me from the beginning (John 15:26-27).

It is always this way: the church and the Spirit must testify to the world. We are to proclaim the gospel, realising that our testimony is in fact part of this twofold testimony.

Divine choice. Human choice. Jesus asserts that both these things need to be heard and taken seriously, otherwise He will continue to be the unheeded Christ.

Did I choose, or was I chosen? The answer to both is, 'Yes.' For Jesus, the truest thing to say is to say two true things.

CHAPTER EIGHT

A FANTASTIC MIRACLE

MATTHEW 17:24-27

In this chapter, we are going to look at a miracle that for many people is an ignored miracle, an unheeded miracle, because it is so fantastic. It is found in Matthew's Gospel, chapter 17, verses 24-27:

> [24]After Jesus and his disciples arrived in Capernaum, the collectors of the two-drachma tax came to Peter and asked, 'Doesn't your teacher pay the temple tax?'
>
> [25]'Yes, he does,' he replied.
>
> When Peter came into the house, Jesus was the first to speak. 'What do you think, Simon?' he asked. 'From whom do the kings of the earth collect duty and taxes – from their own sons or from others?'
>
> [26]'From others,' Peter answered.
>
> 'Then the sons are exempt,' Jesus said to him. [27]'But so that we may not offend them, go to the lake and throw out your line. Take the first fish you catch; open its mouth and you will find a four-drachma coin. Take it and give it to them for my tax and yours.'

Have you ever been embarrassed by what you believe? I can still remember being at Clovelly Primary School in fourth class when, just before the teacher came in, Stephen Smith stood up and said, 'Hey! Cook still believes in Santa Claus!' In fourth class! I was embarrassed. I went home to my parents, in shock that there may not be a Santa Claus. Have you ever been in polite, or even scholarly, academic company, and been embarrassed by what you believe? Perhaps embarrassed by the substitutionary atonement of Jesus? His bodily resurrection? Or what about Jonah's survival in the fish for three days? Or the sun standing still so Israel could wipe out the Amorites? What about those events? They do not embarrass me, but this miracle in Matthew does. There is something about this miracle that is just too fantastic. F. D. Bruner, in his commentary on Matthew's Gospel, calls this an 'embarrassing' miracle.[1]

In Greek mythology, Polycrates was told that in order to appease the Greek gods he had to throw a ring from his finger into the sea. He did that and the gods apparently were appeased. That night when he sat down for dinner and ate a fish, he found the ring he had thrown into the sea in the belly of the fish.

What is this passage about? It begins, in verse 24, with a question from the tax collectors. They ask Peter, 'Is your teacher a tax dodger? Does he pay the temple tax?' The temple tax was not a Roman tax; it was not a civil tax; it was a religious tax. It was levied by the Jewish authorities on all Jewish males, 20 years of age and over, and it was used for the maintenance of the temple. The temple tax was two drachmas per head on each Jewish male, which was a substantial amount. It would represent two days' wages. However, there was no two-drachma coin. The smallest coin was a four-drachma coin, so two men would join together and give one four-drachma coin which would pay the tax for both of them. As well as being a substantial tax, it was

---

[1] F. D. Bruner, *Matthew: A Commentary, Volumes 1 and 2*, (Revised and expanded edition) Grand Rapids: William B. Eerdmans, 2004; Volume 2, *The Churchbook, Matthew 13-28*, p. 204.

a symbolic tax. By paying this tax you showed your solidarity with the Jews, and with the temple, and with God. It became a superstitious tax, because people came to believe that if you paid this tax you were ensuring yourself of health and preservation and of God's blessing on your life.

But the collectors asked Peter, 'Does your teacher pay the tax?' Why should there have been any doubt? Because in Matthew, chapter 12, verse 6, Jesus had said, 'One greater than the temple is here.' The tax collectors want to know, if this teacher says that he is greater than the temple, does he still pay for the upkeep of the temple? Peter responds, in chapter 17, verse 25, by saying, 'Yes, he does, of course he does.' Jesus is not a tax-dodger, even if it is only a church tax.

The second question also comes to Peter. In verse 25, Jesus asks him, 'What do you think, Simon? When the king levies a tax, does he levy it from the prince, from his own son?' Peter responds, in verse 26, 'The king levies a tax from others. So, the princes don't pay tax.' The principle, in verse 26, is that the sons are exempt. Just as princes do not pay tax for the upkeep of the royal household of which they are a part, so Jesus does not need to pay a tax to his Father (who is the Lord of the temple) for the upkeep of the temple (which is the symbol of the royal house). 'My Father,' he is saying, 'is the Lord of the temple and he claims no taxes from me.' Here is a claim to deity, that Jesus is the son of the Lord of the temple. God the Father does not exact payment from Him, because ultimately Jesus is the true temple: he is the meeting place between God and people.

Notice what happens next, in verse 27. Lest the non-payment of the tax be interpreted as a lack of solidarity with God, and with the temple and the Law; lest Jesus cause a scandal or offend people unnecessarily, He says to Peter that he should go and catch a fish. It is the only place in the New Testament where there is reference to fishing not with a net but with a line. 'And the first fish you catch,' Jesus says, 'open its mouth, and you will find the four-drachma coin. Use that four-drachma coin to pay your two-drachma temple tax and mine.'

Notice that Matthew does not even tell us whether Peter carried out his instructions. Matthew is not interested in the sign, he is not interested in the spectacular, but just in the bare word of Jesus to Peter: 'Go, throw in your line, catch your fish, and you will have the four-drachma coin.'

When I was preparing a sermon on this passage, a group of us worked on it in preaching class. In that year's class, we had a student who had written a book on fishing in Brisbane Water. When we talked about the fish having a coin in its mouth, he said, 'It doesn't surprise me at all. I think I could even name what sort of fish would do that.' Drachma coins were often specially minted silver; and the student said to me, 'If you put a lure into the water, you can be sure there are certain types of fish that will be attracted by the shining silver and they'll hit the lure.' He said, 'It doesn't surprise me. I don't think this is a fantastic miracle at all.' Once again, God uses ordinary means to bring about what we would say is extraordinary.

Really, the question we are left with is, 'What does this miracle show us about God? What does it all mean?' One thing it shows us about God is that He is a provider. As commentators have pointed out, Jesus makes the fish His paymaster. God provides for what the temple tax demands. And, of course, as the great provider, He is soon going to provide what the law demands – a perfect life given in sacrifice. He will make that provision through the giving of His Son on the cross.

He is also the great affirmer. Jesus here makes a claim that He is in relationship with the royal household. The Father is the Lord of the temple, and one greater than the temple is here. Peter, in Matthew, chapter 16, verse 16, has said, 'You are the Christ, the Son of the living God.' There is no doubt that when Peter threw in his line and pulled up the fish and found the four-drachma coin, it was underlined to him that Jesus is the Son of the Lord of the temple. He is the unique Son of God.

Matthew alone records this miracle. Why is that? Some have said that whenever money is involved, Matthew is interested. After all, he was the tax collector! But Matthew was writing primarily for a Jewish audience, and he wanted his audience to know that this Jesus, who is the Christ, is the one who stands in unique relationship with the Lord of the temple. He is the unique Son.

Let us look more at the context here. First, go back to Matthew, chapter 17, verse 5. You will notice that chapter 17 begins with what we call 'the Transfiguration'. The disciples are able to glimpse Jesus' eternal glory. At Jesus' baptism there was a direct word from God, and now at His transfiguration there is also a direct word from God. In verse 5, God says, 'This is my Son, whom I love. With him I am well pleased. Listen to him.' This is a magnificent chapter in the way it begins. Now look at the immediate context. In verses 22 and 23, just before this miracle, God's unique Son is speaking to his disciples:

> [22]When they came together in Galilee, (Jesus) said to them, 'The Son of Man is going to be betrayed into the hands of men. [23]They will kill him, and on the third day he will be raised to life.' And the disciples were filled with grief.

There is a divine pattern for kingdom living expressed in this chapter. The exalted, transfigured Son is going to be betrayed and killed, and his followers are going to be grieved. That same pattern of exaltation and humiliation is now duplicated in the miracle we see here. Here is the Lord of all creation – he is Lord over the fish of the sea, he is the Lord over the birds of the air[2] – but in meekness, He does not wish to cause offence. What you see in the transfiguration and in the death of Jesus is majesty and meekness. What you see in this miracle, too, is majesty and meekness in perfect harmony. 'The sons are exempt but – lest we cause offence ...'

---

[2] See Psalms 8 and 104.

Then in chapter 18, Jesus seems to underline this pattern for God's kingdom as He talks about the greatest in the kingdom. In verse 4 He says, 'Whoever humbles himself like this little child is the greatest in the kingdom of heaven.' This is a kingdom that esteems humility and meekness, as in a little child. Then in verse 6 Jesus says, 'But if anyone causes one of these little ones who believe in me to sin, it would be better for him to have a large millstone hung around his neck and be drowned in the depths of the sea.' In verse 10 he says, 'See that you do not look down on one of these little ones.' And in verse 14, 'In the same way, your Father in heaven is not willing that any of these little ones should be lost.' This is a kingdom in which the little ones are the great ones. It is a kingdom of majesty; it is a kingdom of the meek.

When he says, 'the sons are exempt, but lest we offend ...', the Lord Jesus is foreshadowing what He will do on the cross. The Son is free, but He limits His freedom to serve a larger purpose. The Son is free not to pay the tax, but He pays it. The Son is free from sin, death has no claim on Him, but He dies on the cross. He submits, and limits His freedom for the sake of the salvation of the lost. He Himself is God's temple, but He pays the tax to provide for the upkeep of a mere building, lest He offend.

This is a very important miracle. The more I think about it, the more I realise its importance. There is a view amongst some Christians that a mark of true gospel ministry is that it is offensive. And very often, what offends in a gospel ministry is not the gospel itself but the *manner* of the person who presents the gospel. Some would say that here the Lord Jesus is being 'weak'. He is giving in to pressure. Why not offend them? Why not be in their faces? He has every right to say, 'I am the temple, so why should I pay the temple tax?' Instead Jesus shows great sensitivity in verse 27, when He says, 'but so that we may not offend ...'

What is this miracle about? Jesus is giving here a model of responsible exercise of Christian freedom. He is free not to pay the temple tax, yet He pays it. We are free as well. But we are to curb our freedom for the sake of the greater good. Jesus does not want to offend people unnecessarily. He wants to win them to the kingdom, and so he pays the temple tax.

I referred in an earlier chapter to the proverb, 'Eagles don't catch flies.' The eagle has its eye on bigger things. A fly – that's an entrée to the entrée! You don't worry about the fly. Jesus is not concerned about catching flies; He has his eye on the bigger picture. He is not going to risk offending people by failing to pay some tax. He wants people to recognise that He is the Messiah, and to become citizens of His kingdom.

The apostle Paul is like that. In 1 Corinthians, chapter 8, Paul talks about the issue of responsible freedom. In verse 13 he talks about eating meat that has been sacrificed to idols. As an updated example, would you go to a Muslim butcher's shop and buy meat that has been specially slaughtered as the butcher faces Mecca? Paul would say you are free to do it. But having established that principle, he says in 1 Corinthians, chapter 8, verse 13, 'Therefore, if what I eat' – that is, in the exercise of my freedom – 'causes my brother to fall into sin, I will never eat meat again so that I will not cause him to fall.' You see, Paul has got the big picture. The big picture is my brother's godliness; that he keep walking in righteousness. It is not whether I like this meat or not. It is not the exercise of my freedom, but what is good for my brother and his godliness.

Again in 1 Corinthians, chapter 9, verse 12, Paul talks about the exercise of his rights as an apostle. In the second half of verse 12, he says, 'But we did not use this right. On the contrary, we put up with anything rather than hinder the gospel of Christ.' He is talking about whether or not he should draw a salary from the church he pastors at Corinth. But the bigger picture is what is good for the gospel. He draws a salary, or does not draw a salary, depending on what is ultimately good for the gospel. The big issue is the gospel.

In verse 19 of 1 Corinthians, chapter 9, Paul says:

> [19]Though I am free and belong to no man, I make myself a slave to everyone, to win as many as possible. [20]To the Jews I become like a Jew ...to those under the law I become like one under the law ...[21]to those not having the law I become like one not having the law.

His bigger picture is seen in verse 22:

> I have become all things to all men so that by all possible means I might save some. [23]I do this for the sake of the gospel, that I might share in its blessings.

Paul's big picture is that he might identify with people, so as to gain a hearing for the gospel, in order to win some for Christ. These days we might say, 'He is weak. He has lost his evangelical edge. He makes too many compromises.' No. The apostle Paul makes it clear that he has his eye on the big picture, and he exercises his freedom in the light of what is good for the achievement of the big picture, the salvation of people.

F. F. Bruce, in his excellent book *Paul: Apostle of the Heart Set Free*, says, 'A truly free man is not bound to his freedom.'[3] A free man does not always have to act consistently with his freedom. He is free to be paid or not to be paid. He is free to eat the meat or not to eat the meat. And therefore he does not have to always act consistently with the way you think that he should exercise his freedom. He exercises his freedom always in the way he believes best serves the gospel.

When I was in theological college, one of the big issues in those days was the appropriateness of church fairs and church fêtes. With the passage of the years, I can now see why some

---

[3] F. F. Bruce, *Paul: Apostle of the Heart Set Free*, Exeter: Paternoster Press, 1977, p. 202.

churches do not have fêtes, and I can see some good reasons why some churches do have fêtes. It is possible to have a church fête and to use it as an evangelistic event. Keep your eye on the big picture. In questions of whether or not you should be involved in the funeral service of a person who is not a Christian, whether you should marry people together in wedding services who are not Christians, or whether or not to hold church fêtes, we have to exercise freedom. 'What is it that serves the gospel?' is always an important question to guide the exercise of our freedom.

Was the Lord Jesus, in Matthew chapter 17, ready to compromise His principles so as not to offend? No. Just a few chapters later, in Matthew, chapter 21, verse 12, we see that He was not:

> [12]Jesus entered the temple area and He drove out all who were buying and selling there. He overturned the tables of the money-changers and the benches of those selling doves. [13] 'It is written,' he said to them, "My house will be called a house of prayer, but you are making it a den of robbers".

That was offensive! Why wasn't he sensitive about offending people there? Because the integrity of God was being compromised – and Jesus won't allow that to be compromised. The honour and glory of God is the big picture.

Why did Paul argue the way he did in Acts, chapter 15, about circumcision and its non-inclusion in the gospel? It was because the circumcision issue threatened the integrity of the gospel, and therefore, Paul fought hard. As an eagle, he had his eye on the gospel. And then, when that issue was resolved, in the very next chapter he told Timothy to get himself circumcised.[4] This time it was no longer an issue of compromising the gospel, but rather that Timothy's circumcision would be good for the broadcast of the gospel.

Freedom. Do you exercise your freedom responsibly, guided by your greater concern for the gospel and God's honour?

---

[4] See Acts 16:3

In his Reformation treatise *The Freedom of the Christian Man*, Martin Luther wrote, 'The Christian person is the most free lord of all, subject to none. The Christian person is the most dutiful servant of all, subject to everyone.'[5] We reign over all things in Christ. But we reign in order to serve Christ, and to serve the Christ who is in our neighbour. We reign, therefore, in order to be servants.

Now, what is the impossible understanding of this passage in Matthew 17? It is that you and I will insist on exercising our freedom without regard to the effects this may have on both our brothers and sisters in Christ, and also on those who are not yet our brothers and sisters in Christ. I believe that the Lord Jesus would say, 'Take your freedom and press it into the service of the greater good, which is the growth of God's kingdom.' Exercise your freedom with your eye on the big picture, not offending people unnecessarily, but doing all you can, with integrity, to win their allegiance to Christ. Keep your focus on godliness and on what is good for the salvation of people. Exercise your freedom responsibly.

This relates to all sorts of issues at congregational, personal and family-life levels. At the congregational level, you may be part of a traditional church where it is believed that the table where the Lord's Supper is served is somehow an 'altar', and therefore a special holy table. You may see it as just a table like any other, that could be moved, or even sat on, as far as you are concerned. But would it be wise to sit on it? No. The big picture is the salvation of people. Why unnecessarily offend others by the unwise exercise of your freedom - by sitting on the table? If they want to believe it is more than a table, let them believe it. Preach the gospel to them so that they will have a different perspective. But if you go moving the table or sitting on the table without care for them, it may cause them to turn off and not listen to other things you have to say, including the gospel.

---

[5] Martin Luther, 'The Freedom of the Christian Man', *Luther's Works Vol. 31*, cited in D. R. Janz, *A Reformation Reader*, Minneapolis: Fortress, 1999, p. 100.

When we go to Katoomba for the Easter Christian Convention, Good Friday is a day when we share meals with other Christian folk. There are still some fine Christian people, committed Protestants that I know, who do not eat meat on Good Friday but go out of their way to make sure they have fish instead. Now, I don't particularly enjoy fish at any time! I am free in this issue. But why offend people unnecessarily? Eating fish on Good Friday is not a huge compromise, is it? Eat fish on Good Friday – what is the problem? If, in the exercise of your freedom, you know you are going to upset this little one, or the weaker brother in this case, then be careful how you exercise your freedom.

Always – and here is a hint for parenting – always keep your eye on the big picture. Never worry about minor matters. Some of our children have come home from holidays with tattoos. They will flash their tattoos and say, 'So what do you think about that!' I just have to say, 'Oh, yeah, no worries at all.' I have children who have had parts of their body pierced. Again they will say, 'What do you think of that?' When we go to vote as a family, someone will ask, 'How are you going to vote?' One of my children will say, 'Oh, I'm going to vote for the Greens.' Another, 'I'll vote for One Nation.' Another, 'I'll vote for the ALP.' And another, 'I'll vote Liberal.' Tattooed or not tattooed, pierced or not pierced, whoever they vote for, the important thing is that they are in Christ. That is the big issue. That is what you are to keep your eye on as a parent. I don't want to argue about all those other smaller, minor matters, because I want my children to be in Christ, and I want them to be growing to be like Christ and staying in Christ.

Now, it is the same with the exercise of our liberty and freedom. Keep your eye on the big picture. I'm not talking about curbing your freedom in order to compromise: there was no compromise in the temple in chapter 21, verse 12; but there is no unnecessary offence, either. Be careful here, because I think it is true that the mark of a weak person is that every now and then he has to show that he is strong. And the mark of a free person is that they feel every now and then that they must prove they are free. Well, the real mark of a free person is that he or she has nothing to prove about his or her freedom. Therefore, freedom is a gift from God, which is to be exercised carefully, for the good of His people. The Lord Jesus and the apostle Paul had their eyes on the bigger picture – the work of God and winning people to the kingdom.

'Eagles don't catch flies.' I am not to catch flies. Jesus said, 'The sons are exempt, but so that we may not offend ...'. You see, we are to do what Christ did: we are to exercise our freedom, but freedom in the groove, freedom fenced by a desire to serve the greater good of the gospel. Christians sometimes assume that they will begin taking such teaching seriously when they start serving on the mission field or in their local church. A friend of mine in Bible college had on his desk a saying, 'As now, so then'. In other words an unheeded Christ now will be an unheeded Christ then; a heeded Christ now will be a heeded Christ then.

There is no better time to start than now.

Chapter Nine

Resolving Tension

Matthew 18:15-20

In Matthew, chapter 18, verses 15-20, Jesus says:

> ¹⁵ If your brother sins against you, go and show him his fault, just between the two of you. If he listens to you, you have won your brother over. ¹⁶But if he will not listen, take one or two others along, so that 'every matter may be established by the testimony of two or three witnesses.' ¹⁷If he refuses to listen to them, tell it to the church; and if he refuses to listen even to the church, treat him as you would a pagan or a tax collector.
>
> ¹⁸ 'I tell you the truth, whatever you bind on earth will be bound in heaven, and whatever you loose on earth will be loosed in heaven.
>
> ¹⁹ 'Again, I tell you that if two of you on earth agree about anything you ask for, it will be done for you by my Father in heaven. ²⁰For where two or three come together in my name, there am I with them.'

This is a very realistic saying of Jesus, isn't it? First, that wherever two or three gather together in His name, invariably some strife will arise. And second, that in the midst of that, 'I will be with you.' (A fairly loose paraphrase of verse 20, admittedly, but I think an accurate one.)

I can remember one particular day when I was a student minister. It was 15 minutes to service time on a Sunday morning, and I was in the vestry with the minister. The Sunday School superintendent came in and said, 'One of the Sunday School teachers is away.' One of the elders came in and said that the elder who was set down to read the Bible was sick that day. Someone else came in and said that the new vase-stands for the flowers had arrived, but were not identical – one was slightly higher than the other. And then a lady came in and said that the proceeds of the fête had been printed in the church bulletin and should not have been. When everybody left, the minister, giving me a rare glimpse of his true feelings, said, 'I would love the pastoral ministry if it weren't for people!' That's a bit like saying, 'I'd be a great father if I didn't have any children,' or 'I'd be a great teacher if I didn't have any students.'

The fact is that we are imperfect people. The breakdown in communication and relationships that is obvious in our society is unfortunately also obvious in the church itself. But the church is the redeemed community, the community where we are to have substantial restoration in our relationships together. After my ten years of pastoral experience, I believe that if we followed the directions as laid down by the Lord Jesus in these verses, 80 per cent of the pastoral issues I have had to face would not exist. Once before when I shared this statistic, someone corrected me and said, 'No, I believe it would be 100 per cent in my case.' So I guess that if you talked to the majority of pastoral workers they would say that the unheeded Christ is never so unheeded as when He speaks these words in Matthew, chapter 18, verses 15 and following.

If you are offended by a brother, the first step in the process of reconciliation is there in verse 15: 'If your brother sins against you' – that is, if he acts towards you in a way in which his conduct misses the mark, then it is sinful, and his sin offends you or hurts you – 'go and show him his fault just between the two of you.' So, if you have been offended, you must go and explain to him the problem, just between the two of you.

This is difficult because often when our brethren do offend us, we tend to sulk and keep it to ourselves, or we tell others, to get it out of our system. Either response is a sinful response. Jesus says that the reason we are to go to the person who has offended us is not to score points or to encourage him to be sympathetic towards us. We are to go to him in order to win him over, in order to restore the relationship.

Notice that where there is disruption of relationships, the New Testament leaves us no option. If I am hurt, if I am offended, I am to go to the offender. In Matthew, chapter 5, verse 23, Jesus talks about bringing your gift to the altar. He says, 'If you are offering your gift at the altar and there remember that your brother has something against you,' – that is, you are the offender – 'leave your gift there in front of the altar. First go and be reconciled to your brother, then come and offer your gift.' It is always your responsibility. If you have been offended, go to your brother. Or if you realise you have offended, go likewise to the one you have offended. But whether you are the offended or the offender, it is always up to you to take the initiative in restoration.

It is no good saying, 'Well, my brother has done this against me and it has cost me.' The reality is that you are your brother's keeper. When your brother sins against you, because you are in Christ, he is actually sinning against Christ. When your brother sins against you, it puts you out of relationship with him; but at a deeper level, it puts him out of relationship with God, and he may continue in that state until you seek to be reconciled to him. So it is almost as though the reconciliation with you is the first step to your brother coming back into relationship with God. If he really has sinned against you, all sin ultimately, according to David, is against God: 'Against you, you only, have I sinned.'[1] So I am my brother's keeper: I am concerned for his spiritual state.

[1] Psalm 51:4

I may be offended, but I know that behind the offence against me there is a deeper offence, the offence against the honour of God's name.

Jesus says it is just between the two of you – it is not to be spread about. I was on the train going into the city once and I heard the conversation in the seat behind me. It went something like this: 'He – she – it – they – he – she – they – it – they – she – it, etc.' Fortunately the train was so noisy I couldn't catch all the conversation, but only these words. It is never appropriate for us, as Christian people, to be talking about an absent brother or sister in a way that is disparaging towards them.

If you tell anyone else before bringing this offence to the offender, it is a clear breach of verse 15. It is even a breach if you come and say to someone else, 'Look, I don't know whether I should take this to him.' The truth is, you know whether you have been offended or not. You do not need counsel at that point. And it is also a clear breach if you go to your brother and he repents, and then you pass that on to others. There is no need to say, 'Oh, this is what he did to me, but he came to repentance.' Once your brother repents, it is over.

I remember an older Christian man once telling me that if God allows you to know something about a brother or sister that does not reflect well upon them, He does that for three reasons. One, so that you can pray for them. Two, so that you can lovingly go and point it out to them. And three, so that you can avoid the same sin. But never so that you can broadcast that sin to others.

We find the second step in the process in verse 16. Let's say that he doesn't repent, that he won't listen. Jesus says, 'If he will not listen, take one or two others along, so that everything may be established by the testimony of two or three witnesses.' It is at this point that you call in advice. You take one or two others with you. They can bear witness to what is being said; that is the purpose of calling them in. But they can also add weight to your encouragement that your brother should repent. Conversely, they could say to you, 'You are making something out of nothing here. What he has done is not objectively offensive. You need to develop a thicker skin.' That may indeed be the case. But the witnesses are there to add some objectivity to the process.

The third step, if he still continues to resist repentance, is in verse 17. Jesus says, 'If he refuses to listen to them, tell it to the church; and if he refuses to listen even to the church, treat him as you would a pagan or a tax collector.' So if he refuses reconciliation by repentance, tell it to the Christian community; and if he doesn't listen to them, then he is to be treated as an outsider. Treat him as someone who is to be focused on evangelistically, someone who does not have any of the rights and privileges of being in the body of Christ. Martin Luther said that the marks of the true church are that the Word is preached, the sacraments are dispensed and discipline is properly exercised.'[2] Very rarely do we see this sort of discipline today, because salvation is not treated seriously enough, and therefore discipline is often absent.

I hear people say, 'But this is very difficult.' Or, 'This would be an embarrassment.' Or perhaps, 'I attend a Chinese church. It would be almost impossible, where saving face is of paramount importance, to have the congregation discipline someone publicly. It is very, very hard.' But, you see, we need to recognise that the solidarity between Christ and the church is a serious solidarity. In verse 18 Jesus goes on to say that when the church acts in discipline, or even in excommunication, the Lord Jesus will back that up, because sinful behaviour is being rightly addressed and God is being honoured.

In small country towns, people tend to know more about what is going on in one another's lives. People may be known for such things as their business practices or their sexual fidelity. Ask any pastor of a church in a country town whether people may be led to mock the name of God, and the Lord Jesus Christ, if

---

[2] M. Luther, 1539 Treatise on the Councils and the Church, in *Luther's Works: Volume 41*, Philadelphia: Fortress Press, pp. 148-154.

professing Christians in the community are known to be acting with double standards. We need to deal with sin, and we need to be able to talk plainly to each other about sin; and that takes courage. Paul says to Timothy that he is to rebuke, to correct, and to teach. It is easier to teach than it is to correct or rebuke, and that is why I think these words of Jesus are largely ignored and unheeded.

In verse 18, Jesus backs this up with a very significant promise. He confirms in heaven the united activity of His church on earth. He says, 'I tell you the truth, whatever you bind on earth will be bound in heaven, and whatever you loose on earth will be loosed in heaven.' Notice, also, this very precious promise: 'Again, I tell you that if two of you on earth agree about anything you ask for, it will be done for you by my Father in heaven. For where two or three come together in my name, there am I with them.' I believe these promises relate specifically to those who meet to pray and to act in discipline and correction. And you can be sure that when you are seeking to reconcile and win back a sinful brother and you are praying about that with one or two others, having been through this process, Jesus is there with you. He is concerned about the purity and the unity of His church. A concern for purity, and a recognition of the preciousness of Christ's church, leads us to this process of discipline.

Now, let me look at one case study of this principle, and then another which seems to contradict it. In Genesis, chapter 9, we see the account of Noah's drunkenness. You will remember that Noah had three sons, Shem, Ham and Japheth. Noah, we are told, planted a vineyard, and he fell into what you might think was a fairly common temptation for a vineyard owner – he became drunk, and lay uncovered inside his tent. In verse 22 we learn that Ham, the father of Canaan, saw his father's nakedness. He was the youngest son, and with a degree of delight, we gather, Ham told his two brothers outside. Shem and Japheth took a garment, laid it across their shoulders, and then walked in backwards to cover their father. Their faces were turned the other way so that they would not see their father's nakedness, so Noah would not sin against them by his nakedness. When Noah woke up and found out what his youngest son had done, that is, seeing his nakedness and reporting it to his brothers, he said:

> ²⁵Cursed be Canaan! [*that is, the line of Ham*]
>   The lowest of slaves will he be to his brothers.
> ²⁶Blessed be the LORD, the God of Shem!
>   May Canaan be the slave of Shem.
> ²⁷May God extend the territory of Japheth;
>   may Japheth live in the tents of Shem,
>   and may Canaan be his slave.

Why this curse on Ham? Because he broadcast his father's sin. His father was sinful. He had done the wrong thing: he was drunk and naked. Yet here was a son who saw sinfulness in his father and did not go and tell him his fault, but went instead to his two brothers and told them – and he was cursed for it.

Do we find a contradiction to this principle in Galatians, chapter 2? Didn't the apostle Paul know about this teaching of Jesus? The context in Galatians, chapter 2, is that Peter acted in a way that was hypocritical. He had been enjoying table fellowship with non-Jews, but when the Christian Jews came down from Jerusalem, he withdrew from the Gentile believers. Paul says in Galatians, chapter 2, verse 11:

> ¹¹When Peter came to Antioch, I opposed him to his face, because he was clearly in the wrong. ¹²Before certain men came from James [*in Jerusalem*], he used to eat with the Gentiles. But when they arrived, he began to draw back and separate himself from the Gentiles because he was afraid of those who belonged to the circumcision group.

Then in verse 14:

> When I saw that they were not acting in line with the truth of the gospel, I said to Peter in front of them all ...

And then the apostle Paul rebukes Peter's hypocrisy. Now, why did he rebuke Peter like that? Why didn't he take Peter aside privately and show him the error of his ways? Jesus said it should be 'just between the two of you'. But in this case, Peter's sin was quite public, it was quite known, so the public sin of Peter may have led others astray; and public sin requires a public rebuke.

Jesus' word here in Matthew, chapter 18, is a word that takes great courage and strength. It is a very difficult word. Very often in pastoral ministry you will find that people come to the pastor and tell him about the sinful activity of someone else in the congregation, when they have not yet been to that person themselves. Or perhaps you have had the experience of going to a brother who has sinned against you, or sinned against someone else outside the church, and they have demonstrated that the best form of defence is attack. Your brother may well have responded, 'Who are you to talk to me!' and then raise some issue against you. We need to be careful. In a situation where one brother comes in order to achieve reconciliation, it is not the appropriate setting for you to start raising things which you may have against your brother. If you have something to say to your brother, you should do it before he comes to you – but not in a defensive way when your brother has the courage to come to you.

That which unites the church of Jesus is glorifying to God, and substantial restoration between believers is glorifying to God.

In Matthew, chapter 18, the question from Peter follows in verse 21:

> ²¹'Lord, how many times shall I forgive my brother when he sins against me? Up to seven times?'
> ²²Jesus answered, 'I tell you, not seven times but seventy-seven times.'

In other words, there is to be no limit to your mercy. Your forgiveness of your brother is forever and without end. Then

Jesus tells him the story of the man who has been forgiven much but fails to forgive. And the point of the parable is in verse 35: 'This is how my heavenly Father will treat each of you unless you forgive your brother from your heart.' So, if you have been forgiven, and your brother sins against you, God has forgiven far more in you than you are called upon to forgive in your brother. And so you are to forgive completely, from your heart.

Now, the Lord Jesus is giving us these commands and these processes for our own good, so that we will have substantial restoration in our own relationships and not that aching feeling of being out of relationship with one another. How many times had God forgiven Peter? An uncountable number! So, Jesus says, 'Peter, you show the reality of that, by being willing to forgive your brother.'

I read an essay in *Time* magazine in which the writer was saying that when a man is young, he seems to be dominated by lust. When he is middle-aged, the domination comes from ambition for power. And when he is old, he is dominated by anger. Over the years, it is possible to accumulate grudges. People may offend us and we do nothing about it. We accumulate grudges, and unforgiveness and anger builds up.

Now it may well be that you are a very sensitive person and are easily hurt. It may well be that when someone even looks at you the wrong way you feel offended. Be careful lest you bear grudges and become, in your sensitivity, an angrier and angrier person. You need to deal with that. It may well be that you are insensitive, and you love to call a spade a spade, and if that hurts, that hurts; but that's the way you are and people must accept that. If so, you may have brothers and sisters come to you and say, 'You have offended me by your abruptness, and you need to come to repentance about that because that's not the way of Christ.' You must not hide behind the excuse, 'That's the way I am.'

Some Christian groups divide easily because they cannot bring about this sort of reconciliation. Others will not deal with issues, and the division seethes beneath the surface of the congregation for years. We must not ignore this teaching of Jesus. We have standards, and need to see that those standards are upheld. If there is sin, it is ultimately against God. But it shows itself against the individual. It needs to be dealt with at an interpersonal level, and that may even be the route to its being dealt with in relation to God.

Why does the Lord Jesus bother? Why does He talk like this? In the first part of Matthew chapter 18 we see that it is because we are precious to Him. In verse 6 He says, 'If anyone causes one of these little ones who believe in me to sin, it would be better for him to have a large millstone to be hung around his neck and to be drowned in the depths of the sea.' In verse 10 he says, 'See that you do not look down on one of these little ones for I tell you that their angels in heaven always see the face of my Father in heaven.' Be careful of the way you treat others, because they are precious to God and the angels of each one of them have access to God in heaven.

In verse 12 we see that Jesus doesn't just love His church as a whole, but each individual is precious to Him:

> ¹²What do you think? If a man owns a hundred sheep, and one of them wanders away, will he not leave the ninety-nine on the hills and go to look for the one that wandered off? ¹³And if he finds it, I tell you the truth, he is happier about that one sheep than about the ninety-nine that did not wander off. ¹⁴In the same way your Father in heaven is not willing that any of these little ones should be lost.

You see, Jesus doesn't just love His church, he loves *you*. You, singular, are precious to Him. He loves the one wanderer, the one out of fellowship. He loves that one who hurts others by his or her lack of diplomacy. He loves that one who has offended you. Jesus is concerned for them, so do not write them off, do not ignore them. Never give up on people. Go to them and seek to win them back. Persevere with them, hang in there with them, because Christ hung in there for us. Each one of us is precious to Him.

Why does Jesus speak the way He does in verse 15? Because His church is precious to Him, and because He yearns for the purity of His church. He is preparing us for the day when we will be gloriously pure. We are not to ignore sin. We are not to trifle with sin. We are not to let sleeping dogs lie; because if you let the issue lie, it may well be that you are condemning your brother or sister to an eternity without a relationship with God.

Listen to what Jesus says. Then trust Him for the courage to do as He says, lest He remain the unheeded Christ.

CHAPTER TEN

'WHOEVER WANTS TO
BECOME GREAT ...'

MATTHEW 20:20-28

Matthew, chapter 20, verses 20-28 says:

[20]Then the mother of Zebedee's sons came to Jesus with her sons and, kneeling down, asked a favour of him.

[21]'What is it you want?' he asked.

She said, 'Grant that one of these two sons of mine may sit at your right and the other at your left in your kingdom.'

[22]'You don't know what you are asking,' Jesus said to them. 'Can you drink the cup I am going to drink?'

'We can,' they answered.

[23]Jesus said to them, 'You will indeed drink from my cup, but to sit at my right or left is not for me to grant. These places belong to those for whom they have been prepared by my Father.'

[24]When the ten heard about this, they were indignant with the two brothers. [25]Jesus called them together and said, 'You know that the rulers of the Gentiles lord it over them, and their high officials exercise authority over them. [26]Not so with you. Instead, whoever wants to become great among you must be your servant, [27]and whoever wants to be first must be your slave – [28]just as the Son of Man did not come

to be served, but to serve, and to give his life a ransom for many.'

If you knew my son, you would know that he has turned the typically Australian pastime of mocking people good-naturedly into an art form. Once we were visiting my parents, and he decided he would take the opportunity to mock me. So he asked my mother a leading question. He said, 'Granny, did Dad have any ball skills when he was a little boy?' He was expecting the answer, 'No, Daddy was a nerd when it came to sport!' But my mother said, 'Oh, well actually he was a very good cricketer. And he was an excellent golfer. And a very good tennis player. And he had the most natural swimming stroke I have ever seen.' With that last comment, my mother's credibility sank to a new low, because my son knows I'm no swimmer. I was the last to learn to swim in my family. My mother was doing all right mentioning cricket and golf, but when she got to the swimming, I was gone. And my son didn't let me forget it.

That's what mothers are like, isn't it? If you are a son, if you have a living mother, you will know what it is like. A mother loves her son, and my mother loves me. She will defend her son, even before her beloved grandson, who is seeking some advantage in the mockery stakes.

We can feel something of that when we come to Mrs Zebedee. She is concerned for her sons, so she wants them to go to the top. In verse 20 she comes to Jesus, kneels down and asks him a favour. Jesus says, 'What is it you want?' She wants the best positions: 'Grant that one of these two sons of mine may sit at your right and the other at your left in the kingdom. I want one of my sons, please, to be the Deputy Prime Minister and the other to be the Treasurer.' But note also that she is a woman of faith. She is quite clear that Jesus is going to come into His kingdom. She has no doubts about that. And she wants the prime places, after the place of the Lord Jesus, to belong to her sons, James and John.

That is an understandable ambition of a mother for her children. We love our children to be selected, to do well, to be above average. I remember when we first arrived to minister in a country town, we met lots of people telling us that their children were above average. We wondered where the average kids were. And where were the below-average ones, to make up for it? Everyone was above average! We can be very ambitious for our children.

We can also have spiritual ambitions. When I was first ordained into the Presbyterian Church, the most sought-after parish was St Stephen's Presbyterian Church, in the heart of Sydney. Then there were certain other locations which people considered parishes to be avoided. I can remember one elderly minister telling me that they could never fill the vacancies in some of the smaller parishes as long as St Stephen's was also vacant. All the ministers were waiting for the call to St Stephen's, and so no-one would accept the call to a relatively minor parish.

The ambitious request of the mother of James and John comes in the context of verses 18 and 19, where the Lord Jesus says he will be condemned to death, and will be turned over to the Gentiles to be mocked and flogged, and eventually crucified. It's said that when the portrait painter, Sir Peter Lilley, came to paint his portrait of Oliver Cromwell, Cromwell said, 'Paint the portrait well; but don't remark all these roughnesses, these pimples, and these warts. I want you to paint me as you see me.' In verse 20 Matthew realistically paints the raw material with which the Lord Jesus had to deal – ambition, crass ambition. (And notice that Matthew paints himself in this picture, because in verse 24 the ten other disciples are indignant, and one of those ten was Matthew!)

Jesus responds, in verse 22, 'Can you drink the cup?' He is referring here to the cup of God's wrath, the cup of suffering. The way to glory in this kingdom is via the cross. It is via suffering. Jesus said in the Garden of Gethsemane, 'Father, let this cup pass from me.'[1] There are numerous Old Testament references to 'the cup' being the cup of God's wrath, of suffering. The Lord Jesus asks, 'Can you go through suffering?' They lightly respond, 'We can.' And, of course, they would; James was going to be the first martyr of the Twelve, and John was going to be the last. John died of old age, but in exile on the Isle of Patmos. And so the Lord Jesus says, 'You will indeed drink from my cup, but to grant these positions is not for me. It is for my Father to grant this request.'

Matthew tells us, in verse 24, about the indignation of the ten. But they are no better than James and John. They are angry because James and John got in before them! They too wanted the positions of prominence. In Matthew, chapter 18, verse 1, we can see that they had already been discussing this as they were coming up to Jerusalem: 'At that time the disciples came to Jesus and asked, "Who is the greatest in the kingdom of heaven?"' We know from Mark's Gospel that they were debating who was the greatest among them.[2] We see pride and selfish ambition even among those closest to the Lord Jesus.

However, the Lord Jesus does not give up on them. He takes the opportunity to teach them patiently. Isn't it extraordinary that the patience of the Lord Jesus doesn't reach an end? He doesn't say, 'Look, I give up on you blokes.' Rather, he sits them down and teaches them. He contrasts leadership in the world with leadership as it is to be in the kingdom of heaven. He says, in verse 25, 'You know that the rulers of the Gentiles lord it over them, and their high officials exercise authority over them.' The dominant preposition in verse 25 of worldly leadership is the preposition 'over'. That is the nature of worldly leadership: pressing down, oppressing, and dominating – for the selfish ends of the leader.

How might we summarise the worldly leader in verse 25? The worldly leader is The Man. He is the man who defeats all comers in the ring, who's the best on the basketball court, who

[1] Matthew 26:39
[2] Mark 9:33-34

cuts through everyone else on the rugby league field, or in the business or political arena. He is The Man, the champion, because he has trodden on every rival. The Lord Jesus says that this is typical of leadership in the world, but there is to be the clearest contrast between us and the world: 'Not so with you.' In God's kingdom, whoever wants to be first must be a slave. The great one is the servant. Leadership is not oppressive or overbearing. It is not about domination, but it is a matter of service, because the coat of arms in the kingdom of God is the cross of Jesus, and the leadership model of the kingdom of God is service.

This is personified by Jesus Himself. He takes his most exalted title, in verse 28, and says, 'The Son of Man' – who had every right to be served – 'did not come to be served, but he came to serve.' His greatest act of service was that he gave his life as a ransom for many. The Lord Jesus makes it quite clear to these ambitious disciples that in His kingdom, if you want to be first, be last. If you want to live, die. If you want to be king, then be a servant. He gave his life as a ransom – in other words, He drank the cup of God's wrath in order to set us free. He was willing to be pierced for our transgressions, crushed for our iniquities. The punishment that brought us peace was upon Him, and by His wounds we are healed.[3] That was his baptism and the cup He drank.

John (whose mother made this request in v. 21) takes this up in his first letter when he says, 'This is how we know what love is (here is the definition of love): Jesus Christ laid down his life for us.'[4] He became a ransom – that was his great act of service. Jesus not only gives them a lesson in what leadership is to be like in the kingdom, but he models for them what leadership means in the kingdom. The exalted Son of Man goes to the cross, giving up His rights, and giving up His life to ransom many.

What a contrast that is to the 'user' attitude in all of us. In verse 21 what is the question Jesus asks? It is the question of

---

[3] Isaiah 53:5
[4] 1 John 3:16

a servant: 'What is it you want?' Later, in verse 32, when the blind men have a request to make, Jesus says to them, 'What do you want me to do for you?' That is what you would expect a servant to ask. A servant doesn't come and say, 'What can you do for me?' but asks, 'What do you want me to do for you?' Yet, how often do we find ourselves asking the question, 'What can you do for me?' I need to resist the user in me, or what an American writer calls 'the Lord of the Flies factor'.[5] I need to resist it because the Lord of the Flies factor wants to make me The Man. It wants to use others. It wants to rule. It wants to oppress; it does not want to serve. It is possible when you are in Christian ministry – a ministry that involves boldness and authority – to act in a way that can be oppressive, and to use others. Christian ministry can be used to manipulate people. But the Lord Jesus says, 'Not so with you.' You are not to be ambitious in a worldly way. You are not to be seeking the top positions on the right and the left – the mitre on the head, the throne to sit on, the last one in the procession. The Lord Jesus says that is not the way, because the coat of arms of this kingdom is a cross.

Think about leadership in the home. It is not about despotic rule; it is about taking the lead in serving, in doing things that have to be done, which one may not enjoy. The key to the life of a servant is not to do what I like doing, but to learn to like what I have to do. That is the key to being a servant. Make a hobby of what needs to be done, and be a true servant in the home. The leader serves.

When it comes to employment, perhaps you are a person who has been, or who is, an employer of others. Why are you in business? Do you say, 'To make profits so that I can pay dividends to the shareholders'? Might not the servant see that perhaps you are in business so that you can provide gainful employment for other people? Perhaps you could take on that extra person in

---

[5] Editorial, 'The Evil in Us: Prisoner Torture in Iraq Exposes the Ordinary Face of Human Depravity', in *Christianity Today*, July 2004, Vol. 48, No. 7, p 22.

order to give him or her a sense of worth, even though it may reduce your profit margin. Do you recognise that this is an act of service to your workers? 'What do you want me to do for you?' Is that the question you ask?

In an earlier chapter I referred to a quote I keep in the front of my Bible:

> When I reach the end of my days a moment or two from now ... I will consider my earthly existence to have been wasted unless I can recall a loving family, a consistent investment in the lives of people, and an earnest attempt to serve the God who made me. Nothing else makes much sense.[6]

One of the things I love about this quote is the adjectives that are used. Did you notice them? A *loving* family. A *consistent* investment in the lives of people. An *earnest* attempt to serve the God who made me. The Australian Prime Minister, John Howard, came in for some mockery a few years ago when he described himself as 'a cricket tragic'. He is completely absorbed by the game. I love cricket, although I'm not a 'cricket tragic', but I do want to be a *service* tragic. I want always to be looking for ways in which I can serve.

One of the sure ways you can show yourself to be totally out of step with our family is to phone us at the kick-off time for a rugby league State of Origin match, or just as a Bledisloe Cup rugby union match is starting. We would think, 'Who could be ringing up now, when we are all focused on the football? Who could be so ignorant as to ring at a time like this?' Well, one night, sure enough, someone did. I answered the phone, and the caller had a request to make. They wanted me to help them. I thought they mustn't have realised what was about to happen. And the question came to my mind – do I recognise the person of Jesus in this request? 'For as much as you have done it to the least of these my brethren, you have done it unto

---

[6] Dr J. Dobson, http://dvlp.family.org/fofmag/pf/a0029038.cfm

me.'[7] I found it a helpful thought. This is Jesus on the end of the line. A person is making a request for help, and it is actually Jesus making the request, asking me if I can help them. Will I help the Lord Jesus, or will I go back to my trifling sports event?

Are you a servant? One of the ways you can motivate yourself to be a servant is to see that every request that comes to you is coming ultimately from the Lord Jesus Himself. 'For as much as you have done it to the least of these my brethren, you have done it unto me.' This is the Lord Jesus asking me for a glass of water, or a plate of food, or to stay over for the night. Am I going to follow in the way of service?

On Anzac Day[8] a few years ago, one of Australia's Victoria Cross winners, Sir Roden Cutler, formerly the Governor of New South Wales, said that the Australian soldier is renowned for not being good at taking orders. You cannot say to the Australian soldier, for example, 'OK men, out of the trenches and charge to the line.' They are not terribly good at that. But, if you jump out of the trenches as their captain and say, 'Right men, follow me!' you can be absolutely sure, you do not need to look back, they will be following, because Australian soldiers look for leadership and they follow leadership.

Verse 28 tells us that our Lord Jesus leads from the front. 'The Son of Man came, not to be served, but to serve and to give his life as a ransom for many.'

It is good for us to realise that few of us will have opportunities, like Martin Luther, to stand at the Council of Worms and declare our faith before antagonists. Few of us will have the opportunity, like Billy Graham, to pray for the President of the United States at his inauguration. But more frequent opportunities will come to us, like this: 'Can you pick up the tea towel?' 'Can you go

---

[7] Matthew 25:40

[8] ANZAC stands for Australia and New Zealand Army Corps; the holiday occurs on the anniversary of the ANZAC invasion of Turkey during World War I and is an opportunity to honour all military veterans.

and visit that person who is sick in hospital?' 'Can you care for your family, and put off other appointments in order to do so?' 'Can you pick up the phone and call your mother or father, just to let them know you are still here?' 'Can you take the garbage out?' 'Can you wash the car?' 'Can you vacuum the floor?' It may not be praying at the inauguration of the President of the United States, but these are normal, everyday activities, and the Lord Jesus says our energy is to be focused on serving the majestic Son of Man. The Christian secret of the contented life is the secret which the Lord Jesus shares quite openly here. The Christian life is a life of serving others in His name.

It is impossible to come to this section of Scripture and determine that we will follow the way of Christ, but then continue using others. You cannot do that. You need to come to this section of Scripture and say you will follow the way of Christ, which means that at every point you will see yourself as a servant: not lording it over others, but submitting to them. The apostle Paul said, 'Each of you should look not only to your own interests, but also to the interests of others.'[9] To look out for the interests of others, we look out for the interests of Jesus Christ.

It's impressive when the executives of a worldwide fast food chain put on the company's uniform for the day, and serve hamburgers. But the next day, they go back to their plush offices. Yes, it is impressive that they have spent a day with the workers; but the next day they go back to being the master again. The Lord Jesus is actually calling us to a 24-hour, lifetime situation. Serve.

For Christians to live for ourselves instead of serving others would mean that we take no heed of our elder brother, our Lord – the Son of Man who came to serve rather than to be served. Service must run in the family.

The coat of arms is the cross. The motto is service. That is what life is about. So give yourselves to service.

---

[9] Philippians 2:4

CHAPTER ELEVEN

HIS COMING

MATTHEW 24:36-51

Matthew, chapter 24, verses 36-51:

[36]No one knows about that day or hour, not even the angels in heaven, nor the Son, but only the Father. [37]As it was in the days of Noah, so it will be at the coming of the Son of Man. [38]For in the days before the flood, people were eating and drinking, marrying and giving in marriage, up to the day Noah entered the ark; [39]and they knew nothing about what would happen until the flood came and took them all away. That is how it will be at the coming of the Son of Man. [40]Two men will be in the field; one will be taken and the other left. [41]Two women will be grinding with a hand mill; one will be taken and the other left.

[42]Therefore keep watch, because you do not know on what day your Lord will come. [43]But understand this: If the owner of the house had known at what time of night the thief was coming, he would have kept watch and would not have let his house be broken into. [44]So you also must be ready, because the Son of Man will come at an hour when you do not expect him.

[45]Who then is the faithful and wise servant, whom the master has put in charge of the servants in his household to give them their food at the proper time? [46]It will be good for that servant whose master finds him doing so when he returns. [47]I tell you the truth, he will be put in charge of all his possessions. [48]But suppose that servant is wicked and says to himself, 'My master is staying away a long time,' [49]and he then begins to beat his fellow servants and to eat and drink with drunkards. [50]The master of that servant will come on a day when he does not expect him and at an hour he is not aware of. [51]He will cut him to pieces and assign him a place with the hypocrites, where there will be weeping and gnashing of teeth.

Nobody who saw Steven Spielberg's movie, *Saving Private Ryan*, will ever forget the opening scene, when Spielberg depicts the coming of the Allies onto the shores of Normandy. June 6, 1944, commonly known as D-Day, was when the Allies, under the command of General Eisenhower, invaded Europe at Normandy and pressed on through France, finally coming to Berlin. VE-Day – Victory in Europe Day, was declared on May 8, 1945. The success of D-Day made VE-Day and victory inevitable. The eleven-month period between those events was a time of relief because the Allies had come to liberate Europe. While it was a time of hardship as World War II continued, it was also a time of great anticipation for the coming end.

I think we know what it is like to live between two significant events. For example, if you are engaged, you belong to one another; and yet, not quite yet. You are still anticipating the wedding day that is coming. Or you may have been selected to represent your country in a particular sport, and you are in the period between your selection and the game. There is relief that you have been selected, but you are also anticipating the game. It may be that you are elected to office, or called to office, and then you must wait for the induction, or the swearing in. You are living between two significant dates, between D-Day and VE-Day.

The passage we are looking at in Matthew, chapter 24, describes our experience of living between the first and second coming of Jesus. We live between the D-Day and the VE-Day: His first coming makes His second coming, and victory, inevitable. It would be wrong for a person who is engaged to not anticipate marriage. It would likewise be wrong for the church, since we are engaged to God through the work of our Lord Jesus Christ, to have no sense of anticipation for the fulfilment of it all by the coming of God's Son.

Jesus speaks vividly in this passage. He talks about a great separation, He talks about weeping, and He talks about gnashing of teeth. He tells us these things because He loves us. It is only mere sentimentality that does not speak or warn because it does not want to upset. We screen judgment and the reality of heaven and hell out of our consciousness, because it is too threatening for us. But our foolishness is never more evident than when we do not heed the Lord Jesus as He speaks about the future.

Jesus begins, in verse 36, by talking about 'the day'. He says that no-one knows about that day or hour, not even the angels in heaven nor the Son. Only the Father knows. So if the angels do not know, and the Son does not know, then we do not know either.

October 29, 1992, was the day predicted for the return of the Lord Jesus, by a group called the 'Mission for The Coming Days'. The significant thing about October 29, 1992, was that nothing happened. At 3 a.m. that day, when it was expected that Jesus would return, about 300 people gathered at the group's offices in Gladesville, Sydney, waiting for the coming again. But it didn't happen. Members of the media mocked the very idea that there could be an end to this world; they mocked the idea of the coming of Christ. The reality is that although we are in the last days, we simply do not know when it will happen. But we do know it will happen.

What is the indication that we are in these last days? It is that life is going on normally. In verse 38 Jesus says it will be just like the days before Noah entered the ark. People were eating and drinking, marrying and giving in marriage. It was all so normal: they were just living, enjoying life. Their Bible was the *Good Living Guide*. They were not paying much attention to God, but neither were they giving themselves to gross sin. In verses 40 and 41, the Lord Jesus says that the day when the Son of Man comes will involve a separation. Two men will be in the field – a normal, everyday activity – yet one will be taken, and the other left. Two women will be grinding at the mill – a normal everyday activity – yet one will be taken, and the other left. As in the days of Noah, it will be a day of awesome judgment. There will be blessing for some, but separation for others. It will be a day that takes us by surprise.

Jesus goes on, in verse 42, to say, 'Keep watch.' It is a continuous action: we are to keep on keeping watch. In verse 44, he repeats the instruction: 'So you also must be ready.' The Son of Man's coming will be unexpected. Therefore, keep keeping watch; keep being ready; keep on your toes. Every book of the New Testament points to the return of Jesus and urges us to be ready. Be awake, don't be careless.

I remember hearing South African pastor, Frank Retief, speak at a Katoomba Christian Convention about seeking to live by the five-minute rule. That is, whatever is upsetting him now, if he knew Christ were to return in five minutes, would this thing be upsetting him then? He finds that it is a very good corrective to what upsets him and what he judges to be important. Jesus says don't be careless; be ready, be awake, be warned.

Jesus then tells a series of three parables illustrating how we can be ready. The first begins in Matthew chapter 24, verse 45, where the master leaves the servants, and appoints one servant to take charge of the household. The second begins in chapter 25, verse 1, where the bridegroom arrives and is met by the bridesmaids. The third begins further on in chapter 25, verse 14, where the master gives talents to his servants and later returns for an accounting. In each parable an important figure is absent, but then returns and expects people to be ready for him. In the first parable, Jesus is the master leaving his servants in charge of the household. In the second parable, Jesus is the groom coming for his bride. And in the third, Jesus is the master who gives out talents and returns later for an accounting of the gifts he has given.

What I want you to notice in these three parables are the adjectives Jesus uses. In verse 45: 'Who then is the *faithful* and *wise* servant?' Then in verse 48 we have the contrast: 'But suppose that servant is *wicked*.' During the long delay, the wicked one will live comfortably and think to himself, 'Oh, the master is not coming back.' He will indulge himself, thinking that the long delay means he need not continue to be faithful and wise, but instead can be wicked. And Jesus says, in verse 51, 'The master will cut him to pieces and assign him a place with the hypocrites, where there will be weeping and gnashing of teeth.' There is a danger, and Jesus is warning us of it. In the delay, do not let your fitness slide. Be faithful.

When John Wesley was once asked by a friend what he planned to do that day, Wesley said, 'This morning I plan to prepare a sermon, and this afternoon I am going to visit a widow from the parish.' His friend replied, 'If you knew that the Lord Jesus was going to return tonight, what would you do today?' Wesley said, 'I would prepare my sermon this morning and visit the widow this afternoon.' He made no adjustments to his diary, or his lifestyle, in the light of the second coming of Christ. He did not need to. In other words, he was living always in the light of the coming of the Son of Man. In his great book, *The Religious Life of Theological Students*, B. B. Warfield refers to a lecturer in the United States by the name of Philip Lindsay. Warfield said that Philip Lindsay used to tell his students that the best preparation for death, or for the coming of the Son of Man, was a thorough knowledge of the Greek grammar.[1] How about that!

---

[1] B. B. Warfield, *The Religious Life of Theological Students,* Presbyterian and Reformed Publishing Co., 1992, p 4.

You might wish there was an easier way to be ready, but that is the reality. Why? Because Warfield was speaking to theological students. In other words, he was saying the best preparation for death, or for the coming of Jesus, is to do your duty. And the students' duty happened to be a thorough knowledge of the Greek grammar. When the Son of Man comes, you want him to find you doing what He has set apart for you to do. 'Be ready,' Jesus says, 'be faithful and wise.'

Look again at the adjectives, this time in chapter 25, verses 1-13. In verse 4, the distinction between these ten bridesmaids is between wisdom and foolishness. Five of them are wise, and five of them are foolish. The foolish bridesmaids assume it will not be long before the bridegroom comes, so they make no plans for a long delay. In verses 11 and 12, there is an awful finality. Because they do not have enough oil in their lamps, the door is shut and the opportunity is lost. 'Sir, sir,' they say, 'open the door for us.' But he replies, 'I tell you the truth, I don't know you.' They had made no plans to supply themselves in the long delay.

In the first of the three parables there is a long delay, which reveals the self-indulgence of the servant left in charge. In the second parable there is a long delay, which reveals the foolish lack of preparation and perseverance of some of the bridesmaids.

Now we come to the third parable, in chapter 25, verses 14-30. What is required of us in view of the coming of the Son of Man? Should we be passively waiting, looking to the sky? No, it is much more active than that. The master leaves five amounts of money, two amounts of money and one amount of money. Look again at the adjectives. In verse 21 the master says, 'Well done, *good* and *faithful* servant.' Again in verse 23 he says, 'Well done, *good* and *faithful* servant.' Then in verse 26 the master says, 'You *wicked* and *lazy* servant.' Make use of what God gives to you, and he will give you more. Fail to use the gifts God gives you, and you will face the ultimate loss. The last servant was wicked and lazy, and in verse 30 Jesus vividly describes what happens: 'Throw that worthless servant outside, into the darkness, where there will be weeping and gnashing of teeth.' He was created to be good and faithful, but by being wicked and lazy, he was worthless.

What is Jesus saying? He is saying, 'Don't concern yourself about prediction. I will come; all the conditions are now ready.' We are to make faithful use of the gifts God has given us, whether large or small, by serving Him.

Christians are often criticised for being too heavenly-minded to be of any earthly use. I believe that's a myth. I have never met anyone who is too heavenly-minded to be of any earthly use. Rather, I think that when spiritual sensitivities are lost, when hope of the future is blunted, then social services wither away. That can be proven from history. When people lose their grasp on the gospel, they lose their real concern for the needs of others. In my experience, it is Christians – with the clearest view of the future and the freshest expectation of the future – who are the most practical in the way they live in the present.

Let me give you some historical examples of people who had a clear focus on the future. In 1785, a young man was converted. He decided to write a book, which he called a *Practical View of the Prevailing Religious System of Professed Christians, in the Higher and Middle Classes of This Country Contrasted with Real Christianity*.[2] In that book he decided to argue this: that Christianity was not primarily about being good, but it was about the revelation of God's love for us in Christ. His name was William Wilberforce. He did more in the early part of the nineteenth-century to bring about the abolition of slavery than anyone else. He had a clear view of the future, and it affected his living in the present.

In the 1840s a 15-year-old apprentice pawnbroker was converted. He was so concerned about what he saw of the conditions in London that he immediately developed a real burden to help the poor. His name was William Booth, and in 1865, he formed the Salvation Army. What drove Booth and

---

[2] W. Wilberforce, reproduced as *Real Christianity*, Multnomah Press, Portland, 1982.

the Salvation Army? It was a sense of the power of the blood of Christ, the fire of the gospel, and a clear sense of hell, judgment and accountability to come.

In 1895, a lady missionary in Japan was sent home to the UK because of ill health. She couldn't justify staying in the UK, and so in 1901 she went to India, where she noticed that young children were being used as prostitutes in pagan temples. That same year she rescued her first little girl. By the time Amy Carmichael had died, she had rescued hundreds of children from pagan temple prostitution in India. What drove Amy Carmichael? Listen to the poem that drove her.

> Green pastures are before me which yet I have not seen.
> Bright skies will soon be o'er me where the dark clouds have been.
> My hope I cannot measure, my path to life is free,
> My Saviour has my treasure, and he will walk with me.[3]

What drove Wilberforce, Booth and Carmichael to serve in the present? It was a clear grasp of the future. Our problem is not that we are too heavenly-minded to be of any earthly use, but that we are not heavenly-minded enough. We are not looking for the coming of the Son of Man, we do not take it seriously enough, and so we do not give ourselves to passionate, single-minded service in the present.

Before we go any further, notice the setting for these parables and teachings Jesus gives. In Matthew 24, verse 3, we are told that, 'As Jesus was sitting on the Mount of Olives, the disciples came to him privately.' Notice that this teaching of Jesus is given in a private sitting just for the disciples. Listen carefully to what Peter, one of those who was at that private sitting, says about the end times (1 Peter 4:7): 'The end of all things is near.' He then tells us four things we are to do in light of this. *First,* he says, 'Be clear minded and self-controlled so that you can pray.' In other words,

---

[3] 'In Heavenly Love Abiding', Words by Anna Waring, Hymns and Meditations, 1850.

intelligent prayer in the last days is of vital importance. *Second*, in verse 8, he says, 'Above all, love each other deeply, because love covers over a multitude of sins.' Keep working at love, because it feeds forgiveness, and forgiveness establishes our unity. And in these last days there is nothing worse than our being disunited, breaking relationships with one another. *Third*, in verse 9, he says, 'Offer hospitality to one another and don't grumble about it.' The very practical, down-to-earth activity for the last days is to be hospitable to one another. And *fourth*, in verse 10, he says, 'Each one should use whatever gift he has received to serve others, faithfully administering God's grace in its various forms.' Use the talents, the gifts that God has given you, as you face the coming of the Son of Man. What a lovely cameo of life. Are you ready for His coming? Prepare that sermon; visit that widow; do that Greek grammar; cook that meal; pray with those children; continue to persevere in love for that difficult person. That is how we live in a state of readiness – faithfully doing what God has given us to do.

Look again at these words of our Lord Jesus Christ:

I tell you the truth, he will put him (the faithful and wise servant) in charge of all his possessions. (Matt. 24:47)

But while they were on their way to buy the oil, the bridegroom arrived. The virgins who were ready went in with him to the wedding banquet. And the door was shut. (Matt. 25:10)

Well done, good and faithful servant! You have been faithful with a few things; I will put you in charge of many things. Come and share your master's happiness! (Matt. 25:21)

The life of readiness is all about being faithful – not spectacular, just faithful – as we wait for the coming of the Son of Man. That is what will be vindicated and rewarded at Christ's return.

What is the impossible application of this passage? It is impossible to be engaged to God and yet not anticipate the coming of Christ. It is impossible to be a citizen of King Jesus' kingdom and yet live a lifestyle of foolishness, laziness and wickedness.

A friend of mine, who follows such things, tells me that there is a rock band called Green Day. This band have a lead singer known as Billy Joe and they have a song called Warning.[4] In the video of this song, Billy Joe sings about doing everything his mum warned him never to do. He picks up scissors by the blade; he eats raw chicken; he crosses police lines that say 'Don't Cross'; he eats a big meal and then goes for a swim; and he runs along the side of a swimming pool with a sign behind him saying 'Don't Run'. In other words, he is a fool; he lives without heeding the warning. I think that's a great reminder to us. Don't live ignoring Christ's warning. Rather, be a faithful steward with the gifts God has given to you.

Often when I travel elsewhere for ministry, I am impressed by how much we take for granted the rich spiritual resources we have here. The Word of God is central in so many ministries. But I also find that in some other places there is a hunger and appreciation for the Word that we take for granted. We are very rich; God has blessed us in so many ways. We must never take this for granted but instead, in light of living between D-Day and VE-Day, give ourselves wholeheartedly to faithful gospel service.

Our Lord Jesus is never more unheeded than when He talks about the future. Listen to Him and take it to heart.

---

[4] 'Warning', from the album *Warning*, Warner Bros/WEA, 2000.

CHAPTER TWELVE

THE REALITY OF JUDGMENT

MATTHEW 25:31-46

In Matthew, chapter 25, verses 31-46, Jesus says:

³¹When the Son of Man comes in his glory, and all the angels with him, he will sit on his throne in heavenly glory. ³²All the nations will be gathered before him, and he will separate the people one from another as a shepherd separates the sheep from the goats. ³³He will put the sheep on his right and the goats on his left.

³⁴Then the King will say to those on his right, 'Come, you who are blessed by my Father; take your inheritance, the kingdom prepared for you since the creation of the world. ³⁵For I was hungry and you gave me something to eat, I was thirsty and you gave me something to drink, I was a stranger and you invited me in, ³⁶I needed clothes and you clothed me, I was sick and you looked after me, I was in prison and you came to visit me.'

³⁷Then the righteous will answer him, 'Lord, when did we see you hungry and feed you, or thirsty and give you something to drink? ³⁸When did we see you a stranger and invite you in, or needing clothes and clothe you? ³⁹When did we see you sick or in prison and go to visit you?'

[40]The King will reply, 'I tell you the truth, whatever you did for one of the least of these brothers of mine, you did for me.'

[41]Then he will say to those on his left, 'Depart from me, you who are cursed, into the eternal fire prepared for the devil and his angels. [42]For I was hungry and you gave me nothing to eat, I was thirsty and you gave me nothing to drink, [43]I was a stranger and you did not invite me in, I needed clothes and you did not clothe me, I was sick and in prison and you did not look after me.'

[44]They also will answer, 'Lord, when did we see you hungry or thirsty or a stranger or needing clothes or sick or in prison, and did not help you?'

[45]He will reply, 'I tell you the truth, whatever you did not do for one of the least of these, you did not do for me.'

[46]Then they will go away to eternal punishment, but the righteous to eternal life.

You may be tempted to believe media tycoon, Kerry Packer, who said, after having been revived following his brush with death, that there is nothing on the other side. At the memorial service in Sydney for Kerry's late brother, Clyde, the eulogist said of Clyde Packer that he had known that this world was not a dressing room for anywhere else, and so he had lived life to the full. You can choose to entrust yourself to that way of living. Or you can believe our Lord Jesus when he speaks of heaven, hell, judgment, and of a division between the right and the left, the sheep and the goats. What Jesus says seems so crude, though. Surely it is far less threatening, and a more comfortable lifestyle, to go with the Packers.

However, remember that in chapter 24 of Matthew, the Lord Jesus makes it clear that the day of his return is coming. We don't know when that will be. The angels don't know when. Not even the Son knows when the day will come. But we know that it will come, and we need to be ready. He talks about a long delay, and in that long delay, like the five wise bridesmaids, we are to be prepared.[1] Then He tells us how we are to be ready by using the talents, or the gifts, that God has given to us, whether we have been given much or little.[2]

In this passage, Jesus is talking to us about the criterion of judgment on the last day. Notice that life beyond death is assumed, as Jesus says in verse 32: 'All the nations will be gathered before him and he will separate people from one another as a shepherd separates the sheep from the goats.' We can deal with the idea of life beyond death, but what is totally unacceptable is verse 41: 'Then he will say to those on his left, "Depart from me, you who are cursed, into the eternal fire prepared for the devil and his angels".' You see, in our day and age we believe, almost universally, the doctrine of justification by death. The 'In Memoriam' columns of our newspapers will prove my point. All a person has to do to go to heaven today is to die. And everyone who dies goes straight to heaven – justification by death. But Jesus confronts that doctrine here. He says there is a right *and* a left; there are sheep and there are goats. There is an inheritance, and there is an eternal fire in hell.

We may welcome the Lord Jesus to our school speech days to encourage good citizenship. However, when we hear Him as the exalted Son of Man and Judge saying, 'Then they will go away to eternal punishment, but the righteous to eternal life,' we are appalled. What we find here in Jesus is no weak sentimentality. He doesn't back down from mentioning it in case He might offend anyone. Instead He says that judgment is real. The fact that there is a 'right' is real. The fact that there is a 'left' is real. God has no pleasure in the death of the wicked, and neither do we, but we are foolish to ignore these truths.

In one of my parishes there was a Presbyterian ministers' retirement village, and some of the clergy who lived in the village attended our church. I used to publish my sermon series well ahead of time. One particular series I preached

---

[1] Matthew 25:1-13
[2] Matthew 25:14-30

was entitled 'Last Things'. In that series I preached a sermon on 'Hell' and another on 'Judgment'. Noticing that one of the most regular attendees, a retired minister did not come for 'Hell' and 'Judgment', I visited him. He said he was appalled that those subjects should be preached in church. He did not believe in the reality of either. (He thought that the key to a happy ministry was to never be dogmatic.) But it is only irresponsible sentimentality, which tries not to disturb people with the truth. If you blank judgment out of your preaching and out of your thinking, it leads to terrible arrogance, where you believe you can establish your own standards of behaviour. It devalues integrity, because we think we can live for ourselves, without any sense of accountability. And it can cause despair: what is the point of being good? Because whether you are good or wicked, it does not make any difference; there is no accountability. If I forget judgment, it causes me to be apathetic about my personal holiness and about the salvation of the lost.

I mentioned earlier that in these verses Jesus is talking about God's criterion for judgment. What is His criterion? Do we find Jesus here teaching the doctrine of justification by works?

In 2001, there were some interesting responses to what Peter Jensen, the Anglican Archbishop of Sydney, had said about what it means to be a Christian. Radio commentator Alan Jones said, 'When I went to school, we had a headmaster who taught us that if anyone ever asks you "Are you a Christian?" the answer is always, "I'm trying".' It is an interesting comment from a reasonable man. If you answer, 'I'm trying,' and that is all that Christianity is about, then you do not need the incarnation of Jesus, and you do not need the death of Jesus. You do not need Jesus at all if Christianity is simply about trying.

Does Jesus teach here that you will enter into heaven because you have clothed the naked, or looked after the sick? You may know the two questions from *Evangelism Explosion*. The first is, 'If you die tonight, will you go to heaven or hell?' A person will probably answer, 'Heaven'. The second question then is,

'On what basis do you think God will let you into heaven?' If a person answers on the basis of 'I' – for example, 'I have been good', 'I went to church', or 'I gave generously' – these are never appropriate responses. It is only because of Jesus that any of us can enter heaven.

One of my favourite Christian musicians sings passionately about the parable of the sheep and the goats. He sings, 'The difference between the sheep and the goats is the difference between what they did and did not do.'[3] Now, that is only partially true. What is the difference in this parable between the sheep and the goats? Ultimately it comes down to the answer to Cain's question, 'Am I my brother's keeper?'

We will come to that again later, but first let us look at the reality of judgment in Matthew 25:31-33. Jesus says, 'When the Son of Man comes in his glory, and all the angels with him, he will sit on his throne in heavenly glory'. Notice that He repeats the word 'glory'. In verse 32, all the nations will come before the judgment seat of the Son of Man and there will be a separation. Here is a picture of great authority. Notice, it is universal judgment, not universal bliss. Now, it may be difficult for us to tell the difference between a sheep and a goat, but there is no investigation by the Son of Man. We do not come before Him in order that He might investigate; we come before Him to hear His sentence. He knows whether we are sheep or goats. He is astute, so that in verse 34 He is quite clear when He says, 'Come, you who are blessed by my Father'. And again in verse 41, 'Then he will say to those on his left, "Depart from me you who are cursed, into the eternal fire."' He is quite clear. The judge knows the difference between the sheep and the goats.

Now let us give our attention to the sheep in verses 34-40. Notice that they do not earn their inheritance. Verse 34 is quite clear: 'Come, you who are blessed by my Father ...' They are sheep because they are blessed by God. Then the Lord Jesus

---

[3] Keith Green, 'The Sheep and the Goats', from *The Keith Green Collection*, Sparrow Corporation, 1981.

says, 'Take your inheritance, prepared before the foundation of the world.' Even when these sheep were in their natural state of rebellion, God was preparing an inheritance for them. They are blessed. This is an inheritance, a prize, which is unearned. Therefore, eternal life is due to God's blessing, and not due to human achievement. And notice that the reward seems so disproportionate to what they have done. They have clothed the naked, they have cared for the sick, they have visited those in prison, and now they are getting an eternal reward! Just for that?

Now look at what comes out of verses 37-39. 'Lord, when did we see you hungry?' 'When did we see you a stranger?' 'When did we see you sick or in prison?' They are genuinely surprised. It is not as if they did these things to earn a reward. 'Lord, when did we do this? We hadn't noticed.'

The goats are also surprised in verse 44: 'Lord, when did we see you hungry or in prison and did not help you?' They did not recognise their omission. This parable, therefore, centres on verses 40 and 45. What is the criterion of judgment? What will be the determining factor between those on the right and those on the left? In verse 40 Jesus says, 'The king will reply, "I tell you the truth, whatever you did for one of the least of these brothers of mine, you did for me". Then verse 45: 'I tell you the truth, whatever you did not do for one of the least of these, you did not do for me.' The difference between the sheep and the goats is the difference between what they did and did not do for the brothers of Jesus.

The question then is, who are the brothers of Jesus? In Matthew, chapter 12, verse 48, Jesus asks the same question. The context is that Jesus' mother and brothers are standing outside calling for Him. They want to speak to Jesus, but He says, 'Who is my mother and who are my brothers?' That must have been a fairly surprising question. In verse 49, He points to His disciples and says, 'Here are my mother and my brothers, for whoever does the will of my Father in heaven is my brother and sister and mother.' In other words, as the Lord Jesus sees it, there is a strong sense of the spiritual family beyond the physical family. To be a brother of Jesus is to do the will of the Father and therefore to be the Father's son, just as Jesus is *the* Father's great Son.

We find the same answer in Matthew, chapter 28. In verse 7, the angels say about the resurrected Christ, 'Then go quickly and tell his disciples: "He has risen from the dead and he is going ahead of you into Galilee". And in verse 10 Jesus says, 'Don't be afraid. Go and tell my brothers to go to Galilee, there they shall see me.' In verse 7 they are 'disciples', in verse 10 they are 'brothers'. Who are the brothers of Jesus? They are His disciples. Who are the brothers of Jesus? They are those who do the will of the Father in heaven.

I do not have a brother, but I have two elder sisters. I can remember one occasion, when I was about 13 or 14, and I had been encouraged to join a competition tennis team before I was good enough. One week, the captain of the team got up all his courage and rang me on Saturday morning to say I had been dropped from the team. I got off the phone and my middle sister said, 'What's the matter?' I said, 'I've been dropped from the team for this afternoon's match.' She got on that phone – I had never seen this from my sister before – and told the captain, 'How dare you drop my brother from that team.' He was quite right to drop me, of course. But my sister got stuck into him. She's my sister. I'm her brother. If you hurt me, you hurt her. If you hurt her, you hurt me. There is solidarity between us.

Now notice what Jesus says in Matthew, chapter 10, when the twelve disciples are being sent out on mission. In verse 40, Jesus reassures them with these words:

> 40He who receives you, receives me. And he who receives me, receives the One who sent me.

Then in verse 42 Jesus says, 'If anyone gives even a cup of cold water to one of these little ones because he is my disciple, I tell you the truth, he will certainly not lose his reward.'

There is solidarity between the messenger and the Lord Jesus, just as there is solidarity between the Lord Jesus and the One who sent Him. There is solidarity between the Father and the Son, and between the Son and the disciple. So, little wonder that Paul says, 'Do good to all' – have a developed social conscience for all – 'but especially do good to the household of faith.'[4]

In Matthew, chapter 25, verses 35-36, Jesus underlines this solidarity:

> [35]For I was hungry and you gave *me* something to eat, I was thirsty and you gave *me* something to drink, I was a stranger and you invited *me* in, [36]I needed clothes and you clothed *me*, I was sick and you looked after *me*, I was in prison and you came to visit *me*.

And in verse 40 he says, 'I tell you the truth, whatever you did for one of the least of these brothers of mine, I take it as having been done for me.' Now look at verse 42:

> [42]For I was hungry and you gave me nothing to eat, I was thirsty and you gave me nothing to drink, [43]I was a stranger and you did not invite me in, I needed clothes and you did not clothe me, I was sick and in prison, and you did not look after me.

And in verse 45 he says, 'I tell you the truth, whatever you did not do for one of the least of these, I took it as neglect of me.'

What is the criterion of judgment on the last day? Our eternal destiny is determined by how we treat the disciples of Jesus, because how we treat the disciples of Jesus is indicative of how we treat Jesus. To be in relationship with Him is to be in relationship with them. To neglect them is to indicate that we are not in relationship with Him. Whatever we do for them, He takes personally, as if it were done for Him.

---

[4] Galatians 6:10

A few years ago in Macquarie Street, at a workers' protest against the proposed changes to the Workers' Compensation legislation, there was a man who had lost a leg in an industrial accident. He would be affected by this proposed compensation change. There was also an able-bodied worker protesting. Any changes to that affected injured mate also affected him. The workers united will never be defeated. In the same way, there is a great union spiritually between Christ and His people, and between His people, one with another. Remember the words that struck the apostle Paul on the Damascus road, 'Why do you persecute me?'

'But I'm not persecuting you, Lord. I'm only persecuting those Christians.'

'I take your persecution of them personally, as persecution of me.'

That is why the reality that dominated Paul, from that day on, was the preciousness of being 'in Christ'.

Look again at verse 40: 'I tell you the truth, whatever you did for one of the least of these I take it as having been done for me.' There is a similar theme in the Old Testament book of Haggai. Haggai railed against God's people because they had returned from exile and had left God's temple in ruins, but they themselves lived in well-panelled houses. Why is God so concerned about the rebuilding of the temple? Is He concerned about bricks and mortar? No. The temple and its ruin was a symbol of how they had treated God. Just as they had disregarded God, so they had disregarded the temple. Our treatment of one another, as members of the household of faith, is indicative of our relationship with King Jesus, or our lack of it. In Matthew, chapter 25, verses 35-36, the test is how we treat one another when we are at our least attractive – in prison, naked, sick – and when we are unable to acknowledge or repay the help given.

What's the problem with the goats in verse 45? It's that they kept to themselves. 'Whatever you did not do for one of the least of these, you did not do for me.' The parable of the wedding banquet, in Matthew 22, tells us what occupied their time: it was their fields and businesses. They were not grossly immoral, just busy. Work, hobbies, and family were more important to them than the King and his kingdom, and the citizens of the kingdom had no priority for the kingdom in their life. You see, Jesus is not saying, 'Unless you win Wimbledon, you'll never get to heaven. Unless you climb Mount Everest, you'll never get to heaven. Unless you're in the top percentile band for the Higher School Certificate, you won't get to heaven. Unless you're a managing director you won't get to heaven.' He is saying, 'Care for the hungry, care for the sick, visit those in prison who are believers, for as you love me you will love my people.' None of these things is beyond us. To relegate Christian brethren to an inferior position is to relegate Christ. That is why Jesus was so concerned on the cross to say, 'Father, forgive them, because I know that as they are crucifying me, you take that personally.' We should not be surprised then that Stephen, the first Christian martyr, was concerned about that as well. As they were stoning him to death he said, 'Lord, do not hold this sin against them.'[5] When they stoned Stephen, they showed their attitude to the Lord Jesus; and Stephen knew that Jesus would take personally what was done to His servant.

In 2 Timothy, chapter 4, we read some of the last words of the apostle Paul. Speaking of his experience, and reflecting on his life, he says in verse 16, 'At my first defence, no-one came to my support but everyone deserted me. May it not be held against them.' He asks that these actions may not be held against the believers, because when they deserted Paul, they deserted Christ with whom he has solidarity. He learned that on the Damascus road. 'Why do you persecute me?'[6] To persecute the church is to

---

[5] Acts 7:60
[6] Acts 9:4

persecute Christ, and to desert Paul is to desert Christ. 'May it not be held against them.'[7] 'Father, forgive them.'[8] 'Lord, do not hold this sin against them.' Am I my brother's keeper? I certainly am. We need to take our solidarity as seriously as Jesus does.

J. I. Packer in his book, *Knowing God*, sets out this description of what it means to be a Christian. He says:

> I am a child of God. God is my Father; heaven is my home; every day is one day nearer. My Saviour is my brother; every Christian is my brother or sister, too.[9]

Look after other Christians – they are in the family. The way you treat them is a reflection of your relationship, or lack of a relationship, with Jesus.

In 2001, I wrote a letter to a Christian friend who faced financial ruin and long-drawn-out court proceedings. I do not condone what he may or may not have done, but he maintained his Christian testimony, and so I was in solidarity with him. He was weeping and I wept with him, and I wanted him to know that. Twelve months earlier, he had been in a position where he probably could have arranged tickets for me in a corporate box at the Olympic Games! He was not in a position now to do anything; but I was still in solidarity with him because he was in solidarity with Christ, and an indication of my relationship with Jesus was my care for my friend.

'I was hungry, and you gave me something to eat.' Whatever you do for believers in need, who cannot acknowledge, and who cannot repay, the Lord Jesus says, 'I take it personally. Thank you.' Verse 40: 'I tell you the truth, whatever you did for one of the least of these brothers of mine, I take it personally. You did it for me.' Our eternal destiny is determined by how we treat the disciples of Jesus, because how we treat the disciples of Jesus is

---

[7] 2 Timothy 4:16
[8] Luke 23:34
[9] J. I. Packer, *Knowing God*, Hodder and Stoughton, 1973, p. 256.

indicative of how we treat Jesus the Lord, himself. The difference between the sheep and the goats, Jesus says, is the difference between what they did and did not do for one of the least of these brothers of mine.

Do you take your relationship with Jesus so seriously that it bubbles over into your relationships with one another?

CHAPTER THIRTEEN

THE LAST WORD

MATTHEW 28:1-20

Matthew, chapter 28, verses 1-20:

¹After the Sabbath, at dawn on the first day of the week, Mary Magdalene and the other Mary went to look at the tomb.

²There was a violent earthquake, for an angel of the Lord came down from heaven and, going to the tomb, rolled back the stone and sat on it. ³His appearance was like lightning, and his clothes were white as snow. ⁴The guards were so afraid of him that they shook and became like dead men.

⁵The angel said to the women, 'Do not be afraid, for I know that you are looking for Jesus, who was crucified. ⁶He is not here; he has risen, just as he said. Come and see the place where he lay. ⁷Then go quickly and tell his disciples: 'He has risen from the dead and is going ahead of you into Galilee. There you will see him.' Now I have told you.'

⁸So the women hurried away from the tomb, afraid yet filled with joy, and ran to tell his disciples. ⁹Suddenly Jesus met them. 'Greetings,' he said. They came to him, clasped his feet and worshipped him. ¹⁰Then Jesus said to them, 'Do not be afraid. Go and tell my brothers to go to Galilee; there they will see me.'

[11]While the women were on their way, some of the guards went into the city and reported to the chief priests everything that had happened. [12]When the chief priests had met with the elders and devised a plan, they gave the soldiers a large sum of money, [13]telling them, 'You are to say, "His disciples came during the night and stole him away while we were asleep." [14]If this report gets to the governor, we will satisfy him and keep you out of trouble.' [15]So the soldiers took the money and did as they were instructed. And this story has been widely circulated among the Jews to this very day.

[16]Then the eleven disciples went to Galilee, to the mountain where Jesus had told them to go. [17]When they saw him, they worshipped him; but some doubted. [18]Then Jesus came to them and said, 'All authority in heaven and on earth has been given to me. [19]Therefore go and make disciples of all nations, baptising them in the name of the Father and of the Son and of the Holy Spirit, [20]and teaching them to obey everything I have commanded you. And surely I am with you always, to the very end of the age.'

From the beginning, God has purposed to call to himself a people from all nations. Early in the Bible we find this promise:

I will make you into a great nation and I will bless you; I will make your name great, and you will be a blessing. I will bless those who bless you, and whoever curses you I will curse; and all peoples on earth will be blessed through you.[1]

Scripture ends with the same idea:

And they sang a new song:
> 'You are worthy to take the scroll and to open its seals,
> because you were slain,
> and with your blood you purchased men for God
> from every tribe and language and people and nation.
> You have made them to be a kingdom and priests to
>   serve our God,
> and they will reign on the earth.'[2]

---

[1] Genesis 12:2, 3

Throughout Scripture, God calls His people to be a light to the nations.[3] Jesus calls his followers 'light' and 'salt'.[4] Jonah is sent by God to call on the Assyrians to repent. Hosea says that God will call the Gentiles ('not loved one', 'not my people') to be his people.[5] Amos makes it clear that Jews and Gentiles will together make up God's remnant.[6] Luke asserts that it is as much the purpose of God for the gospel to reach the ends of the earth, as it is God's purpose that Christ should suffer and rise from the dead.[7] And one whole book in the canon is given over to showing how God's Spirit-empowered messengers take that all-powerful gospel from Jerusalem, Judea and Samaria to the ends of the earth.[8]

I have begun with this brief background because somehow the idea has grown up that Matthew's great commission is an isolated text, an afterthought, an optional extra. So for this last chapter, I have chosen these words of Jesus as a final example of how he is unheeded.

The great commission is under assault from many quarters today. It is under assault by the elevation of tolerance and pluralism, which assert that people (outside of Christ) are better left alone, happy in their own religious expression; by the attitude that seeks to excuse our failure to take the gospel overseas, by asserting that the world has come to us instead, in multicultural Australia. It is under assault from the healthy concentration on local evangelism, which can so easily develop into an unhealthy neglect of our worldwide responsibilities. And it is under assault from our natural desires for comfort and security, because it is hard to be separated from our family, friends, culture, and our accustomed lifestyle.

---

[2] Revelation 5:9, 10
[3] See, for example, Isaiah 42:6 and 49:6
[4] Matthew 5:13-16
[5] Hosea 1:10 and 2:23
[6] Amos 9:11, 12
[7] Luke 24:46, 47
[8] Acts 1:8

In Matthew, chapters 27–28, Jesus has been crucified, then buried in the tomb of Joseph of Arimathea. The tomb is secured and guarded to prevent the theft of the body and the pretence of resurrection. When the women come to the tomb, there is an earthquake: an angel messenger says to the women that Jesus has been raised, that they must go to tell His disciples, and they will see Jesus in Galilee. They then see Jesus and worship Him before going to Galilee. Meanwhile, the guards who shook before the angel and became like dead men had told the chief priests everything that happened, and the priests in turn bribed the guards to say that Jesus' disciples stole His body. It is against the background of this evidence, and the varied reaction of those involved, that Matthew now gives his account of the great commission.

Hearing the testimony of the women, the disciples went to Galilee as instructed by the angel and Jesus. There they saw the resurrected Lord, the one who died and was now risen, having made no concession to death. Even at that magnificent moment, however, there was a divided response. Some worshipped, as the women had in verse 9; and yet in verse 17, some disciples doubted. Was it that this event was just too extraordinary to be believed? Could their eyes have been playing tricks on them? If only these doubting disciples had been able to read the following from Blaise Pascal in the seventeenth-century:

> What reason is there for saying that we cannot rise from the dead? What is more difficult – to be born or to rise again; that what has never been should be or that what has been should be again? Is it more difficult to come into existence than to return to it? Habit makes the one appear easy to us; want of habit makes the other impossible.[9]

Jesus' resurrection was inevitable. Peter says in Acts, chapter 2, verse 24, 'But God raised him from the dead, freeing him from the agony of death, because it was impossible for death to keep

---

[9] Blaise Pascal, *Pensées*, III, 222.

its hold on him.' Paul, in 1 Corinthians, chapter 15, verse 20, says, 'But Christ has indeed been raised from the dead, the firstfruits of those who have fallen asleep' – the firstfruits of a mighty harvest to follow.

Matthew, chapter 28, verse 18, tells us 'Jesus came to them'. It was the same as He had done at His transfiguration, where Matthew, chapter 17, verse 7, records, 'Jesus came and touched them'. No doubt he came to reassure the doubters that it was the real Jesus, and not some ghost. Here then, in verses 18-20, are the words of the risen Lord Jesus Christ:

> [18]Then Jesus came to them and said, 'All authority in heaven and on earth has been given to me. [19]Therefore go and make disciples of all nations, baptising them in the name of the Father and of the Son and of the Holy Spirit, [20]and teaching them to obey everything I have commanded you. And surely I am with you always, to the very end of the age.'

He is the one with *all* authority in *every* sphere. The disciples are to go to *all* nations, they are to teach *everything*, and the authoritative Lord will be with them *always*. It is the repetition of the comprehensive 'all' that gives this commission its adjective – the *great* commission.

This is an entirely consistent word for Matthew's hearers. It is very similar to Isaiah's brilliant prophecy that is found in Isaiah chapter 66, verses 19-21. How are the nations going to be blessed by God's great act of salvation? God will send some of His people from the remnant of Israel, to distant nations 'that have not heard of my fame or seen my glory. They will proclaim my glory among the nations.' As a result of God's messengers going out to all the nations, there will be a great in-gathering of people to Jerusalem.

It is Jesus who enables the fulfilment of Isaiah's prophecy. He establishes salvation, and as the Lord with all authority, he commissions his disciples to go and 'make disciples of all nations'. That is, they are to introduce people from every nation to Jesus, so that they become His followers.

The basis of Jesus' commissioning derives from what He says about Himself. He says that He has all authority in every sphere. He has the whole world in His hands. Yet He says that this authority has been 'given' to Him. By whom has it been given? It has been given by God, because God alone has authority. Yet Isaiah chapter 42, verse 8, says that God gives His glory to no other. Thus, here we see that Jesus is divine. He is part of the Godhead. The Father gives all authority to the Son.

Because of Jesus' universal lordship (v. 19 begins with 'therefore' or 'so') the clear implication is that the disciples of Jesus are to go and claim the nations of the world for their rightful Lord.

How are they to do this? In verses 19 and 20, the original Greek (in which Matthew's Gospel was written) has a familiar construction. There is one command: 'You (*plural*) make disciples'. This one command is surrounded by three dependent participles: going, baptising, and teaching. (Similarly, in Ephesians, chapter 5, verses 18-21, the one command, 'Be filled with the Spirit', is followed by five dependent participles: speaking, singing, psalming, giving thanks, and submitting. The participles are an explanation of the command, they show how the command is to be fulfilled. To 'be filled with the Spirit' therefore involves speaking, singing, psalming, thanksgiving and mutual submission.) Likewise, to make disciples involves going to where the potential disciples are, baptising them and teaching them to be obedient to the gospel. It is by our doing these things that God through His Spirit will make disciples.

So, firstly, we are to be *going*. We are to reach out into every nation with the gospel so that God may call His disciples. Only God knows who, out of all people, will be His. Acts, chapter 18, verses 9-11 give us a clear illustration of this:

[9]One night the Lord spoke to Paul [*who was then in Corinth*] in a vision: 'Do not be afraid; keep on speaking, do not be silent. [10]For I am with you, and no-one is going to attack and harm you, because I have many people in this city.'[11] So Paul stayed for a year and a half, teaching them the word of God.

God knew those who would be His. Paul's role was to present them with the gospel so they would hear God's call.

Secondly, the disciples of Jesus are to be *baptising*. It is as though Jesus is saying that by baptism, the public sign of repentance, people are deposited into the account of the triune God – Father, Son and Holy Spirit. Baptism is a symbol of being joined to Christ. Such a depositing comes by means of repentance and faith. You will recall Peter's words on the Day of Pentecost in Acts, chapter 2, verses 38-39:

> [38]Repent and be baptised, every one of you, in the name of Jesus Christ for the forgiveness of your sins. And you will receive the gift of the Holy Spirit. [39]The promise is for you and your children and for all who are far off – for all whom the Lord our God will call.

Baptism is a means of grace whereby the church affirms that those who are baptised have been joined to God: they are no longer Adam's, but now they belong to Christ and are infused with God's Spirit.

Baptism itself does not bring about this union with Christ, so why does Jesus include it in his commission? It's because baptism indicates to both the disciple and the world that, through the gospel, the disciple has been brought into union with the saving work of the Son. Through this, the disciple enjoys the oversight and care of the Father and the empowering companionship of the Holy Spirit.

Thirdly, we are to be *teaching*. Up until now, Jesus has been the teacher. His disciples were made through His teaching.

New disciples are to be made through the disciples' teaching. And notice it is not teaching with a view merely to a growth in knowledge. It is teaching that produces daily obedience to all that Christ taught.

These three activities – going, baptising and teaching – are all involved in what it means to make disciples of Jesus.

In Romans, chapter 8, verse 29, Paul reminds the believers at Rome that God's one agenda item for them is that 'they be conformed to the image of his Son'. 'To disciple' is the verb Jesus uses to express the one agenda item that comprises all the missionary responsibilities of a believer. It is through going out, baptising and teaching that we are to bring people into fellowship with Jesus and help them to grow in their likeness to Him. This growth will cause them to follow Him in the way of service, for, as Matthew, chapter 20, verse 28 says, 'The Son of Man did not come to be served, but to serve, and to give his life as a ransom for many.'

The reason the believers are to do this is because the cosmic Lord has commissioned them to see that people rightfully recognise His rule. Psalm, chapter 2, verse 8, makes it clear that the nations are His rightful possession: 'Ask of me, and I will make the nations your inheritance, the ends of the earth your possession.' So the apostles are commissioned to go and bring the nations to the rightful recognition of their Lord.

Some might query whether Jesus' commission was a commission for the twelve alone, or whether it includes us as well. The emphasis on the boundless scope of Jesus' lordship would indicate that these words are to be taken as a relevant commission for us. Jesus, God's Christ, always has all authority. His commission therefore never 'runs out'. The fact that the promise of verse 20 is to the completion of the age would indicate that the relevant commission that accompanies such a promise is of similar duration, 'to the completion of the age'. Christ's words are to be taken to apply to his whole church.

It's important to note that these verses are not isolated. They are not one-offs: in fact the whole thrust of Scripture is for the people of God to be a declaring people. In 1 Peter, chapter 2, verses 9-10, we read:

> [9]But you are a chosen people, a royal priesthood, a holy nation, a people belonging to God, that you may declare the praises of him who called you out of darkness into his wonderful light. [10]Once you were not a people, but now you are the people of God; once you had not received mercy, but now you have received mercy.

Until we gather around the triumphant Lamb and sing the song of Revelation 5, verses 9-10, we must continue to be a declaring people.

Jesus describes the events which will bring about the completion of the present age. In Matthew, chapter 24, verse 3, his disciples ask the question, 'Tell us, when will this happen, and what will be the sign of your coming and of the end of the age?' Jesus makes it clear, in verses 30-31, that the completion will be when the Son of Man comes.

> [30]At that time the sign of the Son of Man will appear in the sky, and all the nations of the earth will mourn. They will see the Son of Man coming on the clouds of the sky, with power and great glory. [31]And he will send his angels with a loud trumpet call, and they will gather his elect from the four winds, from one end of the heavens to the other.

Then the last judgment will happen.[10] His commission and its accompanying promise apply to all who are His, until He returns and the last judgment takes place. It is indeed a great commission, which continues until the great judgment day.

Christ's precious promise that He will be with the disciples follows in verse 20. In the original Greek, the order is even more graphic – literally, 'I, with you, I am, all the days.' The presence of

---

[10] Matthew 25:31-46

the risen Lord will surround the gospel-bearers. The particular reference of this promise is for the missionary, the one who proclaims the gospel – just as the promise of Matthew, chapter 18, verse 20, 'For where two or three come together in my name, there am I with them', has particular reference for those who seek to win back the sinful brother. What a wonderful promise this is: to know that, even though discipling may be tough and difficult, the one with all authority is our companion, surrounding us always until our work is done. This promise of Matthew 28:20 sustained David Livingstone throughout the perils of his life in Africa. This promise from Jesus Christ, he said, '... is the word of a gentleman of the most strict and sacred honour, so there's an end of it!'[11] With that he got on with his work. Jesus' promise has sustained many others in ministry, as well.

In verses 18-20, there is a sandwich-type structure to the commission of Jesus. There is His authority in verse 18, the commissioning in verse 19, and the promise of His presence in verse 20.

Since the reaching and discipling of all nations is the commission of the church, how can we encourage the church to be more focused on the task? I believe we can begin by first disbanding all church mission committees. In each church I have pastored, there has been an active mission committee, which has sought to encourage interest in mission in the life of the church. But if mission, and the great commission, is to be at the core of the church's being, then everything the church is to do, without exception, must relate to its missionary outreach. Mission is the most vital task of the church and it must dominate all discussion and planning. The central leadership body of the church must then be the mission committee. So the choice is either to disband the mission committee or to make it the central decision-making body of the church. The church leadership must ask the questions: How does every activity of

---

[11] From David Livingstone's diary, 14th January, 1856; quoted in F. W. Boreham, *A Bunch of Everlastings, or, Texts That Made History*, New York: Abingdon, 1920.

our church facilitate the movement of the gospel outside the church walls into our society and on to the ends of the earth? How are we encouraging people to go? How are we freeing them up to baptise and to teach?

The danger of so many people training for ministry here in Sydney, wonderful as that is, is that they will stay and serve churches in Sydney. It is as though Australia is surrounded by nations that are starving because of a food shortage, while our farms are producing more and more food for us. Imagine if our leaders were to urge us to eat more and more, so as to use up our surplus food supplies. We would not tolerate such selfishness and inequality in the distribution of food, so why do we tolerate such selfishness and inequality in the distribution of spiritual resources?

We have a responsibility to all nations. In Romans, chapter 1, verse 14, Paul could say he had an obligation to all nations and to all classes of people within those nations. 'I am bound both to Greeks and non-Greeks, both to the wise and the foolish.'

The church at Antioch is a model for us, to take our best people and send them out to needy lands:

While they were worshiping the Lord and fasting, the Holy Spirit said, 'Set apart for me Barnabas and Saul for the work to which I have called them.' So after they had fasted and prayed, they placed their hands on them and sent them off.[12]

We need to resist the temptation to create bigger and bigger ministry teams if that means that we are cutting back on sending out missionaries to the hopelessly dark lands where Christ's rule is not recognised.

The Heidelberg Catechism, in Question 65, asks:

Question: It is by faith that we share in Christ and all his blessings; where then does this faith come from?

Answer: The Holy Spirit produces it in our hearts by the preaching of the holy gospel.[13]

---

[12] Acts 13:2, 3

[13] Question 65, *The Heidelberg Catechism*, CRC Publications, Grand Rapids, 1989.

Faith comes by hearing, says Paul.[14] How shall they hear unless someone preaches to them? And how shall they preach unless they are sent?[15]

This is Christ's manifesto. It is the natural outcome of His rightful claim to have been given all authority.

Christ is tragically unheeded – He is robbed of the glory due to Him from the nations – when we ignore the commission to go to the lost, wherever they are. 'I have many people in this city,' God says. 'I have many people in the megacities of South-East Asia, the plains of Central Asia, the jungles of South America, the commercial centres of Europe, the vast masses throughout Africa. I have many people in this city.'

Before Adoniram Judson[16] left as a pioneer missionary, he wrote to the father of Ann Hasseltine (known as Nancy) asking for his daughter's hand in marriage:

> I have now to ask, whether you can consent to part with your daughter early next spring, to see her no more in this world; whether you can consent to the departure and her subjection to the hardship and suffering of a missionary life; whether you can consent to her exposure to the dangers of the ocean; to the fatal influence of the southern climate of India; to every kind of want and distress, to degradation, insult, persecution, and perhaps a violent death. Can you consent to all this, for the sake of him who left his heavenly home and died for her and for you; for the sake of perishing, immortal souls; for the sake of Zion, and the glory of God? Can you consent to all this, in hope of soon meeting your daughter in the world of glory, with the crown of righteousness, brightened with the acclamations of praise

---

[14] Romans 10:17
[15] Romans 10:14, 15
[16] Adoniram Judson (1788–1850) was an American Baptist missionary, lexicographer, and Bible translator to Burma.

which shall redound to her Saviour from the heathens saved, through her means, from eternal woe and despair?[17]

John Hasseltine gave his daughter the freedom to make up her own mind. Adoniram and Nancy were married. They sailed for the mission field. Nancy and both of her children died in Burma, and Adoniram lost a second wife and two more children there. It was 'for the sake of him who left his heavenly home and died for her and for you; for the sake of perishing, immortal souls; for the sake of Zion, and the glory of God.'

As you read the history of the church, you will find many such examples, disciples of the Lord Jesus, heeding the commission to go. The world will offer every reason to stay: 'Get more training'; 'You have an intimate knowledge of the language and culture here'; 'This is your home'; 'Get security in the real estate market now'; and the One with all authority will remain unheeded.

Make disciples – going, baptising, teaching – and He is with us to the end!

---

[17] Courtney Anderson, *To the Golden Shore: The Life of Adoniram Judson*, Valley Forge: Judson Press, 1987.

HOW TO SPEAK AT
SPECIAL EVENTS
FOREWORD BY DAVID COOK

How to Speak at Special Events
Foreword by David Cook

Communication is such a vital part of today's world – we are bombarded with thousands of media-transferred messages every day. But with thousands of messages comes confusion. Clarity when talking of ideas and concepts are rare.

Public speaking, as exemplified by politicians, has become the science of sound bites for that 5-second media slot. Communication in today's society is not equipping us for public speaking.

Christianity communicates ideas that need to be thought through, contemplated and reflected upon. Christians use words because God uses words. He is interested in verbal and written communication. He communicates ideas about himself primarily to us in his written word, the Bible.

So if you are faced with an event or occasion when public speaking is needed you may find yourself in need of a helping hand.

How to speak at special events can help – because it is written by experts in their field.

But before you can prepare an effective talk, you have to prepare yourself and your material. It's not just a case of throwing some jokes and Bible stories together and hoping. *How to speak at special events* will guide you step-by-step along the way.

If you want to make an effective impact at a special event then you need *How to speak at special events*.

Contributors:

Rev Dr Sam Chan

Canon John Chapman

Rev Stuart Coulton.

Mr Jonathan Dykes

Bishop Dudley Foord

Rev Ray Galea

Mrs Sandy Galea

Rev Simon Manchester

Rev Richard Newton

Ms Jenny Salt

Ms Sue Steele-Smith

Rev Grant Thorp

Dr Leigh Trevaskis

ISBN 9781845502775

TEACHING
ACTS

Unlocking the book of Acts
for the Bible Teacher

DAVID COOK

SERIES EDITORS: DAVID JACKMAN & ROBIN SYDSERFF

Teaching Acts:
Unlocking the book of Acts for the Bible Teacher
David Cook

Published in conjunction with The Proclamation Trust

There are commentaries, and there are books on preaching – but very few books that are specifically geared to the preacher or Bible teacher tackling a series on a Bible book or doctrinal theme.

Key features of books in this series are introductory chapters on 'getting our bearings in the book' and 'planning a series'. The 'meat of the book' then works systematically through a suggested series, working with the Bible teacher from text to sermon or talk. Each chapter ends with a suggested preaching / teaching outline and a detailed Bible study which would be ideal for small groups.

Books in this series are aimed at developing confidence in handling God's Word in a variety of contexts. Whether you are a preacher, a small group leader or youth worker, these books will give you the necessary tools for teaching.

Teaching Acts is a welcome addition to the series. Acts is a tough book to teach, but vital to the church in every generation.

ISBN 9781845502553

DAVID**JACKMAN**
WILLIAM**PHILIP**

PROCLAMATION
TRUST MEDIA

TEACHING**MATTHEW**

unlocking the gospel of matthew for the expositor

Teaching Matthew:
Unlocking the Gospel of Matthew for the Expositor
David Jackman

Matthew's Gospel is a substantial book to consider teaching through - its large sections on teaching and theological reflection seeming to predominate over the 'action' of the story.

However, precisely because there are such rich seams of theology, and so much teaching from Jesus himself, it is a wonderful treasure-trove.

It also excels as a way of explaining the message of the New Testament gospel so as to open up a sense of its continuity with the whole Old Testament, and the fulfilment of God's covenant promises in Jesus Christ. This is not an exhaustive exposition of the Gospel. The major focus is on Matthew's five great teaching sections. It is not intended to take the place of commentaries but complement them, as few commentaries seem to be written with the sermon (or Bible exposition) as the point of reference that is being worked towards.

As we work through Matthew's Gospel, then, the aim is to help the Bible teacher find a way into the text that will enable him to use it for its given purpose: to be proclaimed as the living word of God. That is the point of Scripture, what it is meant for.

ISBN 9781857928778

TEACHING
I PETER

Unlocking the book of I Peter
for the Bible Teacher

ANGUS MACLEAY

SERIES EDITORS: DAVID JACKMAN & ROBIN SYDSERFF

Teaching 1 Peter
Angus MacLeay

There are commentaries, and there are books on preaching – but very few books that combine elements of both to enable the preacher or Bible teacher to prepare and present a series on specific sections of scripture.

This series gives the Bible teacher suitable tools to understand the context of Biblical books; doctrinal themes; the methods of interpretation; the key teaching points and how to deliver that message to the audience.

Whilst very useful for preachers, this book is also aimed at enabling youth workers and small group study leaders have the confidence they need to teach Biblical principles and doctrine.

Teaching 1st Peter looks at the first letter from the Apostle Peter to a primarily gentile audience scattered around Asia Minor. Angus enables the leader to explain the context of this letter and it's relevance to a contemporary setting where gentile Christians are surrounded by a pagan culture.

He also enables the leader to apply practical theology to specific situations that still affect the church today. This is the latest addition to the Teaching the Bible series.

Angus Macleay is the minister of St. Nicholas, a large Anglican Church in Sevenoaks, and is also a member of the Church of England General Synod. One of St. Nicholas' previous ministers was the poet, John Donne. The recent story of the church is told by the book 'The Church that went under'.

ISBN 9781845503475

Oliver Claassen

Lifesong

Bible-centered Worship
for the Emerging Generation

Lifesong:
Bible-centered Worship for the Emerging Generation
Oliver Claassen

Pure worship is declaring with our words and lives that God is more important to us than anything else – that he is our deepest desire and that he is worth more than anything else we hold dear. God alone is worthy of worship because he alone is righteous.

Louie Giglio points out that worship is simply about value. Our worship is a response to what we value most. It is easy to identify what we value most by the things we do. If we consider that a person, a thing, or an experience is what matters most then we are willing to sacrifice in order to get it. Worship is coming before the "throne" of what is of ultimate value to us.

In the Old Testament the priests would build an altar on which to offer the sacrifices to the One whom they worshipped. Everyone who is willing to sacrifice has first to build an altar. In order to find your altar of worship just follow the trail of how you use your time, energy, money and affections. The more time you spend before that throne, the more your life will reflect what or whom you worship. Our actions speak louder than our words.

In the New Testament the priestly sacrifice is described as "Through him [Jesus].." (Heb 13:15) - and it is Jesus himself who warns us by saying, "Not everyone who says to me Lord, Lord, will enter the kingdom of heaven, but he who does the will of my Father who is in heaven." (Matthew 7:21).

Dr. Oliver Classen is the Senior pastor of the Evangelical Presbyterian Church, Cape Coral, Florida

ISBN 9781845503734

Christian Focus Publications

publishes books for all ages

Our mission statement –

STAYING FAITHFUL
In dependence upon God we seek to help make His infallible Word,
the Bible, relevant. Our aim is to ensure that the Lord Jesus Christ is
presented as the only hope to obtain forgiveness of sin, live a useful
life and look forward to heaven with Him.

REACHING OUT
Christ's last command requires us to reach out to our world with
His gospel. We seek to help fulfil that by publishing books that point
people towards Jesus and help them develop a Christ-like maturity.
We aim to equip all levels of readers for life, work, ministry and
mission.

Books in our adult range are published in three imprints.

Christian Focus contains popular works including biographies,
commentaries, basic doctrine and Christian living. Our
children's books are also published in this imprint.

Mentor focuses on books written at a level suitable for Bible
College and seminary students, pastors, and other serious
readers. The imprint includes commentaries, doctrinal
studies, examination of current issues and church history.

Christian Heritage contains classic writings from the past.

Christian Focus Publications Ltd
Geanies House, Fearn,
Ross-shire, IV20 1TW, Scotland, United Kingdom
info@christianfocus.com

Our titles are available from quality bookstores and
www.christianfocus.com